"Integrity manifests itself at both the [...] age where opportunities seduce many, [...] a commodity for leaders, for managers, and for us all as we steward whatever we find in our hands. Rollie offers actionables for both the heart and the hands. I recommend this book and even more so the message it summons us to."

—HEATH ADAMSON, Senior Director of Youth Ministries,
Global Chairman WAGF Next Gen Commission,
Author of *The Bush Always Burns*

"Once again, my friend Rollie Dimos has provided vital help for pastors and local church leaders in his new book, *Integrity at Stake: Safeguarding Your Church from Financial Fraud*. Rollie's clear and engaging style offers valuable insights and recommendations that will keep ministry leaders from the tragedies others have experienced. Healthy churches manage their finances in careful and healthy ways. In this book, Rollie covers all the bases and will show you how to address each of the primary financial responsibilities you must manage. A must-read for every church treasurer and for the pastors who lead them!"

—MICHAEL CLARENSAU, DMin, Dean for
the College of Bible & Church Ministries,
Southwestern Assemblies of God University

"Integrity is a nonnegotiable. When an organization's trustworthiness comes under question because of faulty systems or fraudulent action, the consequences are devastating. Whether you find yourself leading in a church, parachurch, or nonprofit, you owe it to your organization to read *Integrity at Stake*. The stories Rollie tells and the insights he provides will give you valuable keys to protect your organization's God-given influence."

—JOHN LINDELL, Lead Pastor,
James River Church, Ozark, Missouri

"Dimos has delivered an essential and informative resource for the church. A must-read for anyone concerned about biblical stewardship."

—PAUL R. MCDONALD, District Treasurer and
Business Administrator, Assemblies of God,
Northern Missouri District

"Over the years Rollie has proven himself as one of the brightest minds and most qualified in the area of church and nonprofit fraud prevention. Several years ago our ministry opened our books to Rollie to gain his wisdom and knowledge in the area of ethical financial reporting and protection. His input was invaluable! I wholeheartedly endorse Rollie's new book, *Integrity at Stake*, as a resource for any church or ministry that is interested in managing with integrity the Lord's resources."

—DON K. WIEHE, Executive Secretary Treasurer,
South Texas District Assemblies of God

"I highly recommend that church leaders and church boards obtain Rollie Dimos's book *Integrity at Stake: Safeguarding Your Church from Financial Fraud*. I have worked personally with the author and know firsthand of his outstanding expertise on this subject. If an ounce of prevention is worth a pound of cure, then in this book you will receive far more than an ounce of prevention! If the counsel given in this book is followed, your church will be well protected from financial fraud."

—GEORGE O. WOOD, General Superintendent,
the General Council of the Assemblies of God

"*Integrity at Stake* is well done and greatly needed. I particularly found the statistics from accounting firms to be interesting. I felt that the tips were clear and precise to help prevent fraud. And the case studies played to my 'curiosity factor' to see who did what and how."

—DR. MARK WOOTTON, Professor at
Evangel University, Pastor, and Church Planter

Integrity at Stake

Integrity at Stake

SAFEGUARDING YOUR
CHURCH FROM
FINANCIAL FRAUD

ROLLIE DIMOS

ZONDERVAN

Integrity at Stake
Copyright © 2016 by Rollie Dimos

This title is also available as a Zondervan ebook. Visit www.zondervan.com/ebooks.

Requests for information should be addressed to:
Zondervan, 3900 *Sparks Dr. SE, Grand Rapids, Michigan* 49546

Library of Congress Cataloging-in-Publication Data

Dimos, Rollie, 1967-.
   Integrity at stake : safeguarding your church from financial fraud / Rollie
Dimos.
      p.   cm.
      Includes bibliographical references.
      ISBN 978-0-310-52500-4 (softcover)
      1. Church finance. 2. Fraud. I. Title.
BV774.5.D56   2016
254'.8 — dc23   2015028636

Any Internet addresses (websites, blogs, etc.) and telephone numbers in this book are
offered as a resource. They are not intended in any way to be or imply an endorsement
by Zondervan, nor does Zondervan vouch for the content of these sites and numbers
for the life of this book.

Cover design: Bradford Foltz
Cover photography: CTRd. Getty Images
Interior design: Kait Lamphere

Printed in the United States of America

15 16 17 18 19 20 21 22 23 24 /DHV/ 20 19 18 17 16 15 14 13 12 11 10 9 8 7 6 5 4 3 2 1

For my wife and best friend, Tammy. Thank you for being my biggest fan and cheerleader. I couldn't have accomplished this book without your constant support and encouragement.

For my parents. As leaders in the church, you consistently modeled accountability, transparency, and integrity.

For my wonderful kids, Aaron and Taylor. You make me smile every day, and I'm so proud to be your dad. You are amazing miracles, and I love watching you both grow in God!

CONTENTS

SECTION ONE
Fraud: A Frank Discussion on the Potential Risks to Your Organization

SECTION TWO
Case Studies: True Stories of Fraud and Practical Ways to Prevent It

FOREWORD

THE CHURCH, parachurch ministries, and nonprofit organizations are designed to be conduits of hope and rays of light that result in the transformation of people's lives. However, when an organization neglects good stewardship practices, it can lead to fraud and financial abuse. When this occurs, it diminishes that ministry's Kingdom influence.

There have been some improprieties that are so acute that the government is actually wondering if churches and nonprofits are complying with the law. All of this causes the church and the ministry to lose credibility and ultimately its ministry effectiveness.

If there is one thing better than a minister of a church or a CEO of a nonprofit organization publicly admitting mistakes and asking for forgiveness, it's NOT having to have a public reading of transgressions!

My friend and colleague, Rollie Dimos, has devoted his life to helping Christ-centered organizations earn and maintain high levels of trust through developing high standards of accountability and practice. He gets it ... both the ministry and management!

Integrity at Stake is not a fictional book. These are actual situations that caused financial setbacks and were embarrassing to the ministry. Interestingly, each of these could have been avoided if greater accountability and transparency were embedded in the ministry's policy and practice.

Caution: The subject material in this book may prevent you from experiencing any fraudulent schemes in the ministry you lead!

—Doug Clay | General Treasurer
The Assemblies of God National Leadership and Resource Center

INTRODUCTION

THE BIBLICAL PATRIARCH JOB understood adversity. He knew despair. He had experienced loss of health, loss of family, and loss of fortune. In the midst of unfathomable grief and loss, his wife and friends were encouraging him to turn his back on God. However, Job didn't waver in his convictions. He understood his character was on the line.

His integrity was at stake.

Job was pressured to compromise, but he stood firm in his convictions and didn't sin against God. He maintained his integrity, and he maintained his honor.

I've been involved in the financial operations of various churches and nonprofits for almost twenty-five years. From performing the bookkeeping, to being elected treasurer, to providing consulting services to pastors and boards as an internal auditor, I've been involved in all aspects of a ministry's financial operations. I've served alongside ministries with good financial practices, and I've been able to help other ministries improve poor practices.

But over the years, I've seen people who, unlike Job, compromised their integrity and committed financial abuses. Abuses that included:

- Pastors and bookkeepers writing church checks to pay for personal expenses for their family and friends
- Church staff using the church credit card for personal charges
- Pastors hiding unauthorized transactions from the board
- Ministry leaders transferring funds to secret bank accounts
- Churches having to close their doors because they failed to send their payroll taxes to the IRS

The world is suffering an economic crisis—and our churches are not immune to this crisis either. We often think that fraud only happens on Wall Street; but, sadly, it also happens on Main Street—in the midst of our churches.

We may think of organizational fraud as a victimless crime since the organization isn't a real person and companies should have sufficient funds to recover the loss. However, when fraud occurs in the church, significant spiritual ramifications linger long after the financial effects have passed. The church will have probably lost some funds, but financial abuse performed by a spiritual leader can ruin the leader's ministry and possibly destroy a church, leaving a building full of people whose faith has been shattered in its wake.

Misuse and abuse of ministry funds occur due to the lack of accountability—in some of the cases mentioned earlier, accountability was virtually nonexistent.

I encourage churches to embrace accountability and transparency, two essential keys that will minimize risk and help your church fulfill its mission. By adding a few simple internal controls, you will increase the accountability and transparency of your nonprofit organization, bring integrity to your financial operations, and in my opinion, characterize biblical stewardship!

But everyone in the church must embrace accountability and transparency. These two keys must be part of your church culture and DNA. Most importantly, they must be modeled by your leadership. Remember, pastors, as you model accountability and transparency in your churches, your staff, church board, and congregation will follow!

Over the next few chapters, I will discuss the importance of accountability in your ministry's financial operations and reveal the impact that poor controls have had on various churches and nonprofits. I pray that as you read through this book, you will understand how embracing accountability and transparency will help the success of your ministry and protect your church from financial fraud.

WHO SHOULD READ THIS BOOK

WITHIN EVERY ORGANIZATION, someone has the primary task of managing the organization's finances. No matter the title — bookkeeper, accountant, treasurer, or chief financial officer — these people have the day-to-day responsibility of receiving income, paying bills, recording transactions, and preparing financial reports. Certainly, they also have a responsibility to make sure assets are safeguarded and proper controls are in place to minimize the risk of fraud.

However, this book is also written for many others within the organization who are charged with the responsibility to steward nonprofit resources and prevent the misuse and abuse of donor funds, including:

- Pastor/President. As pastor, you may also fulfill the role of president, chairman of the board, or chief executive officer. You probably don't count the offering, make deposits, or post transactions into the financial records, but you decide when and where funds are spent. You also have the authority to bypass established policies, which sometimes circumvents controls. This book is for you, to help you realize the importance of implementing and enforcing a system of internal control.
- Treasurer/Chief Financial Officer. Your role includes managing the financial operations and providing reports on the

current status of finances. It is important for you to know financial controls are in place and operating effectively.

- Accounting Staff. Whether your title is accountant, bookkeeper, finance specialist, or accounting clerk, you handle the day-to-day financial transactions for the organization. The accuracy and integrity of the organization's finances rest with the accounting team.

- Deacon/Board of Directors. Your role, as the governing board, includes making sure finances are managed effectively while propelling the organization forward in fulfilling its mission. You'll want to make sure segregation of duties and other financial controls are in place to safeguard the organization's assets while protecting the integrity of the organization and its staff.

Essentially, every employee in the church or nonprofit ministry plays a part in preventing fraud. No matter your title or role, this book will reveal how fraud can occur in churches and other nonprofit organizations and how you can prevent it.

FRAUD

*A Frank Discussion on
the Potential Risks to
Your Organization*

ONE

FRAUD RISK: WHAT EVERY LEADER NEEDS TO KNOW

FACING THE FACTS

You might have read this headline in 2009: "Father and Son Pastors Plead Guilty to Stealing $3.1 Million from Church."[1] Or maybe you read about the pastor who embezzled $700,000 from his congregation,[2] or that $1.3 million designated for church planting was misused by pastors.[3]

Many times, we think that fraud only happens in large corporations like Enron or WorldCom, but it can happen to small nonprofit organizations too. Unfortunately, many religious and charitable organizations may think their organizations aren't at risk because they employ people who, they feel, possess strong moral and ethical convictions. Others may erroneously believe that strong controls require additional staff and great expense. As a result, leaders let their guard down and fail to implement processes with strong controls that ensure accountability.

One of the most frequent abuses in church finances is using nonprofit funds for personal use by stealing cash from the offering plate, writing unauthorized checks, or using the church credit card for personal expenses. External pressures such as personal debt, medical crisis, or an unexpected job loss can cause even the most loyal employee to make a rash and unfortunate decision. These perpetrators may rationalize their actions by thinking of the theft as just a temporary loan, fully intending to pay it back. Others justify their actions because they feel underpaid or undervalued and believe they are owed the extra pay.

In 2014, the Association of Certified Fraud Examiners examined 1,483 fraud cases, of which 10.8 percent occurred at nonprofit organizations.[4] First-time offenders, with no prior criminal convictions, perpetrated the fraud in 95 percent of all cases.[5] For those nonprofit organizations that experienced fraud, the median loss was $108,000.[6]

If a fraud occurs, the church will lose more than just money. Donor confidence will rightly be weakened, and they may decide to reallocate their contributions to other organizations. Further, the reputation of the church and its pastor in the local community could be permanently damaged.

Can your church afford a loss of this magnitude? More importantly, do you know how to protect your organization from fraud?

INTEREST FROM ALL SIDES

Accountability and transparency shouldn't be exercised just for the donors in the pews. These safeguards are also important to the many other organizations watching you. Certainly, donors want to make sure their contributions to a particular ministry are used responsibly and further the ministry's stated goals, but external interests also monitor the accountability and good governance of nonprofits.

Media and watchdog groups keep a keen eye on nonprofit activity to ensure it is transparent and responsible. State attorneys general are interested in protecting the funds donated by their constituents, and the IRS requires that nonprofits comply with appropriate rules and regulations for tax-exempt groups. In fact, from 2002 to

2012, the percentage of tax-exempt returns examined by the IRS has doubled.[7]

Congress also watches to make sure religious organizations are accountable and compliant to maintain public confidence in the nonprofit sector. In January 2011, Senator Chuck Grassley, ranking member of the Committee on Finance, released a report on the review of activities and practices of media-based ministries, churches, and other religious organizations. Characterized as an ongoing effort to strengthen the tax-exempt sector, Grassley said his goal was to improve accountability and governance of tax-exempt organizations in order to maintain public confidence.[8]

WHY ACCOUNTABILITY MATTERS

Oftentimes, I meet church leaders who are fearful of making their financial activity accountable and transparent, and many times, control of the church's finances is limited to one or two individuals. In a best-case scenario, this is simply an honest but naïve mind-set, believing that finances are better controlled when fewer people are involved. In a worst-case scenario, this is a deliberate attempt to conceal poor stewardship or abuse. It's the worst-case scenario that will ruin a leader's ministry, destroy a church, and shatter people's faith.

A prominent preacher once lamented publicly that accountability is just a code name for red tape. He stated that it was simply a tool for accountants and bureaucrats to question a leader's decisions and a backdoor approach for stopping progress. It was apparent this leader wasn't a fan of accountability and transparency. Unfortunately, a few years later, this leader learned that his associate pastor had embezzled $700,000 from the church. The associate pastor's decision to steal from the church was his own choosing; however, the lack of accountability in the organization was certainly a contributing factor.

This type of situation can be avoided by embracing accountability—and by realizing that accountability is a scriptural principle!

The principle of accountability runs throughout the Bible. In scriptural terms, accountability means giving an account of how well we steward the gifts and resources that God gives us. The Parable of the Talents is an example of how God holds us accountable for our stewardship (Matthew 25:14–30). Additionally, as described in the Book of Revelation, each person will stand before God and give an individual accounting of their lives on the Day of Judgment (Revelation 20:11–15; see also Romans 14:12).

Paul even addresses the accountability of his work in his letter to the Corinthian church. He wrote: "We want to avoid any criticism of the way we administer this liberal gift. For we are taking pains to do what is right, not only in the eyes of the Lord but also in the eyes of man" (2 Corinthians 8:20–21).

In business terms, church leaders are the stewards of an organization's resources, including all funds received from donors. Pastors and board members are accountable to one another for the business decisions they make. And they are all accountable to their donors for how well they steward contributions.

In practical terms, without accountability, human nature tends to drive us to the dividing line between right and wrong, where we encounter the gray areas of life. Certainly, making right choices involves listening to the leading of the Holy Spirit; but it also involves submitting ourselves to others and seeking wise counsel. The Book of Proverbs reminds us that "in the multitude of counsellors there is safety" (Proverbs 11:14 KJV).

In today's world, leaders feel pressured to follow the latest trends and buzzwords. They are strongly encouraged to try new things, push the envelope, think outside the box, and engage the current culture and ideas. Ideas are not intrinsically evil; in many cases, they may be necessary to foster a growing and thriving congregation. But failing to submit oneself to another's accountability creates opportunity to cross the line into misuse and abuse.

Accountability and transparency of financial operations aren't meant to constrain leaders; instead, they are meant to protect leaders and the reputations of their organizations. If I could paraphrase that verse from Proverbs in financial terms, it would say: Where there is a multitude of counselors *who discuss, review, and approve the financial operations of the church*, there truly is safety.

INTERNAL CONTROL AND RISK MANAGEMENT

FORGING A STRONG DEFENSE

The economic downturn in recent years has affected many organizations' ability to meet their business goals. Maybe you were an employee of a manufacturing company who experienced production cutbacks, reduced hours, layoffs, or even termination. Maybe you have family members or close friends who have experienced a recent job loss. Undoubtedly, the economic condition has affected many of us.

But what about churches and other nonprofit organizations? How has the economic crisis affected them? More importantly, has the country's economic downturn impacted the risk of fraud in our churches? Consider these statistics:

- A survey published in 2013 by the Leadership Network found 50 percent of churches were negatively impacted by the economy in recent years. Not surprising, they discovered church size was directly proportional to the amount of negative impact experienced. For example, 67 percent of churches with less than 1,000 in attendance were negatively impacted by the economy.[1]

- A recent study of fraud events identified in 2013 found that 60 percent of fraudsters were motivated by a desire to increase or maintain their standard of living.[2]
- Another study of frauds investigated between 2012 and 2013 determined that the perpetrator experienced financial difficulties in 33 percent of the cases and was characterized as living beyond their means in 43.8 percent of the cases.[3]

These statistics reveal the real risk that our churches face. Financial pressures on our church members mean increased pressure in our churches. Strong internal controls are an effective defense to the increased risk of fraud in our churches, and they are a key component of risk management.

Simply put, risk management is the process of identifying, evaluating, and responding to uncertainties (i.e., corporate risk) that could jeopardize an organization's ability to achieve its business objectives.

To understand why risk management is important to your organization, consider two key terms in that definition: corporate risk and business objectives.

Corporate or business risk refers to potential sources of trouble that businesses face. These are the types of risks that, if they occurred, would impact the success of your organization. Unfortunately, churches are not immune to corporate risk, which could include:

- Not meeting ministry goals
- Misusing designated funds
- Using nonprofit funds contrary to IRS regulations
- Financial misconduct by staff
- Reduced contributions (through increased economic pressure on donors or by losing donor confidence and trust)

Business objectives are those short-term and long-term goals that define how your organization will achieve its mission. Together, these objectives help create a road map for the future. Here are some examples of a church's business objectives:

- Accountable and transparent operations
- Biblical stewardship of donor resources
- Strong donor confidence
- Safeguarded assets

Business objectives may be perpetual (never-ending), as in the examples used above; or they may be short-lived, such as, "increase capital funds by 10 percent in twelve months."

You may find the business objectives of a local church in its mission statement, or they may be found in a list of the church's core values. For example, the mission statement of the Assemblies of God Fellowship is to fulfill the fourfold mission of the church: evangelism, worship, discipleship, and compassion. Further, the fellowship will fulfill this mission by committing to the following five core values:

- Passionately proclaim Jesus as Savior
- Strategically invest in the next generation
- Vigorously plant new churches
- Skillfully resource the church
- Fervently pray for God's favor[4]

While the fellowship implements these five core values, they will need to effectively identify, evaluate, and respond to various uncertainties and risk factors that could hinder their ability to achieve its fourfold mission.

The success of the business objectives and core values of your organization will also be directly affected by your organization's response to risk. Our challenge as leaders is to first identify the risks and then decide on a plan of action to manage controllable risks and minimize those that are uncontrollable.

This is the relationship between risk management and internal controls. Your organization's system of internal control is your first line of defense to combat the risks that could hinder the success of your mission.

FINDING HOLES IN THE DEFENSE

A survey completed by KPMG International, a global network of professional firms providing audit, tax, and advisory services, found in 2011 that 74 percent of the fraud cases that they reviewed occurred by exploiting weak internal controls.[5] KPMG theorized that, due to a downturn in the economy, many organizations had to cut costs to balance their finances. These cost-cutting measures resulted in less robust controls and few resources to monitor those controls. This allowed fraudsters to exploit the weaknesses.

Unfortunately, the average fraud in North American companies occurred repeatedly for over four years before being detected, and the average loss exceeded $1.2 million.[6] In 96 percent of these cases, the perpetrator conducted repeated fraudulent activity, which raises the questions of whether the controls for detecting and preventing fraud were effective and whether management was performing adequate oversight.[7]

For nonprofits, the statistics are just as alarming.

The Association of Certified Fraud Examiners' 2014 *Report to the Nations* is a must-read for church leaders who are interested in minimizing the risk of fraud and embezzlement in their organization. From January 2012 to December 2013, the ACFE reviewed 1,483 cases of worldwide occupational fraud. Here are some interesting findings from the report:

- The typical organization loses 5 percent of its revenue to fraud each year.
- The median loss for fraud cases reviewed was $145,000, but 22 percent had actual losses greater than $1 million.
- The smallest organizations in the study suffered larger median losses; they had the least amount of antifraud controls, making them more vulnerable to fraud.
- Fraud committed by owners and executives was significantly larger than frauds committed by managers and employees.
- In 92 percent of the cases, fraudsters exhibited behavioral red flags, such as living beyond their means, experiencing financial difficulties, or had unusually close relationships with customers or vendors.[8]

Unfortunately, churches and ministry organizations are not immune to fraudulent activity. Of the 1,483 fraud cases reviewed, 10.8 percent occurred within nonprofit organizations.[9] The median loss for nonprofit organizations was $108,000 while strictly religious and charitable organizations experienced a median loss of $80,000.[10]

Oftentimes, fraud schemes are difficult to detect and usually involve people who you'd least suspect. According to the ACFE, fraud schemes lasted a median of eighteen months before being detected.[11] And in 95 percent of all cases reviewed, the perpetrator was a first-time offender with no prior criminal conviction and 81.7 percent had a clean employment history.[12]

However, strong internal controls and other accountability measures can help detect fraud sooner. For those organizations that had implemented various internal controls, the frauds were detected sooner and resulted in less monetary losses. The ACFE found:

- 42 percent of frauds were uncovered through tips.
- 30 percent of frauds were uncovered by internal reviews (management reviews and internal audits).

- 11 percent of frauds were uncovered by reconciling accounts and examining support documents.[13]

Somewhat surprisingly, the ACFE determined only 3 percent of frauds were uncovered by external audits.[14] Unfortunately, I find many churches rely on a financial statement audit as their only fraud detection tool.

Some of the characteristics discussed above are the very reasons that our churches are at risk for fraud. Churches often have only one or two people involved in the accounting and bookkeeping functions. Financial controls are usually vested in just one or two people. Budgets are tight, so fewer resources are invested in strengthening financial controls. Often, the pastor has significant authority and influence over financial activity.

The ACFE study revealed that small businesses, like churches, are particularly vulnerable to fraud. The ACFE determined that organizations with fewer than 100 employees had the greatest percentage of reported fraud cases, and concluded:

> Small businesses are both disproportionately victimized by fraud and notably under-protected by anti-fraud controls, a combination that makes them significantly vulnerable to this threat.[15]

Similarly, in a previous study, the ACFE commented about the impact of fraud in small businesses, stating:

> These organizations typically have fewer resources than their larger counterparts, which often translates to fewer and less-effective anti-fraud controls. In addition, because they have fewer resources, the losses experienced by small businesses tend to have a greater impact than they would in larger organizations.[16]

The ACFE estimates that typically 5 percent of an organization's revenues are lost to fraud.[17] The cost of fraud is particularly harmful to small organizations like churches, where the actual impact will not only include finances, but a damaged reputation and a loss of donor confidence. In 2012, public charities reported over 1.65 trillion dollars in total revenues.[18] If 5 percent is lost to fraud each year, this equates to over 82.5 billion dollars lost to fraud in 2012. Think about the magnitude of that statistic: Public charities lost access to over 82.5 billion dollars that couldn't be used to further their charitable causes here and around the world.

The good news is that the organizations that implemented any number of common antifraud controls experienced lower losses than organizations that didn't implement these controls. The duration of the fraud was considerably less as well.[19] The implication for churches is clear: Even though they may have fewer resources at their disposal, churches and other nonprofits must implement measures to reduce the risk of fraud in their organizations. Strong controls like segregation of duties, robust reviews and approvals, and transparency are a must.

DEFINING INTERNAL CONTROL

Have you heard the phrase "inspect what you expect"? When discussing U.S. relations with the Soviet Union, President Ronald Reagan often quoted a similar Russian proverb, *"Doveryai no proveryai,"* or "trust, but verify."[20] These phrases succinctly convey the role internal control plays in minimizing risk within nonprofit organizations.

According to COSO,[21] internal control is a process to provide reasonable assurance that an organization will have:

- Effective and efficient operations
- Reliable financial reports
- Compliance with applicable laws and regulations[22]

Everyone would probably agree that these are three great business objectives for the local church. But they are not confined to the finance and accounting function; they encompass the broader business goals of the organization.

One of the most important financial controls within an organization is the segregation of duties. This is a key component of internal control that involves multiple people. This is especially important when handling cash. I like to summarize this control as requiring two sets of eyes on every transaction — from collecting and counting the offering, to recording the deposits, to paying the bills. A system of internal control also includes establishing goals and objectives, creating operating policies and procedures, organizing and training staff, etc.

Internal control helps ensure that the "business of ministry" is successful. In other words, internal control is a process for managing risk!

TAKING OWNERSHIP

In the nonprofit world, the purpose of internal control is to increase the accountability, transparency, and integrity of financial operations. This goes hand in hand with the biblical theme of stewardship.

Unfortunately, sometimes leaders view internal controls as roadblocks or obstacles, but remember, many nonprofits are vulnerable to fraud or abuse because they have a weak system of controls. Let me challenge your thinking and submit to you that a system of internal control actually helps promote biblical stewardship of God's resources! Internal control will reduce the risks of financial loss, the risks of not meeting business goals, and the risks of losing donor confidence.

In my experience, two key causes of weak controls are prevalent in our churches today: poor segregation of duties and frequent override of established policies and procedures. These can be easily overcome — and without significant cost, additional staff, or time.

But it requires that the leadership recognize the importance of, and commit to, strong controls.

Think about your church or ministry organization and answer these questions:

- What is the ethical climate of your organization (i.e., "tone at the top")?
- Do your leaders typically make exceptions to policy or follow policy?
- Are accountability and transparency practiced at all levels of your organization?

Internal control is only effective as a risk management tool if everyone is supporting it, including the president and board members, full-time staff, and part-time staff. From the boardroom to the mailroom, everyone is responsible for internal control.

Let me encourage you to practice accountability through the implementation of strong internal control processes. This will include publicly embracing accountability, documenting specific internal controls in your policies and procedures manuals, and embedding this theme throughout your organization's DNA. I said this earlier, but it is worth repeating again: Pastors, as you model accountability in your churches, your staff and congregation will follow!

Later in this book, I'll discuss several real-life examples of how weak systems of internal control contributed to fraud and abuse in different ministry organizations. (While all of these stories are true, the names of the individuals and organizations involved have been changed to protect their identities.)

If you find your organization is similar to one or more of these case studies, having similar processes and practicing weak controls, I'll provide several ways to implement additional measures that will improve controls and reduce the risk of fraud within your organization.

CHAPTER THREE

MOVING FORWARD AFTER FRAUD

THE CONSEQUENCES OF FRAUD

Fraud is not a victimless crime; all of the frauds discussed in this book were not harmless acts but had dire consequences for the defrauded organizations. If your church has been a victim of a fraud, you are well aware of these consequences.

As previously stated, when fraud occurs in the church, there are spiritual consequences as well as financial. The church can lose more than just money. It can end up ruining a leader's ministry, destroying a church, and shattering people's faith. It also impacts the organization's ability to perform ministry and meet the needs of others.

Consider the consequences that the following organizations faced:

- One church that was the victim of a $712,000 embezzlement scheme by their office manager had to cut employees' pay by 10 percent and cancel a benevolence assistance program for their members.[1]

- A Catholic archdiocese that was defrauded of one million dollars by its accounts payable clerk had to close churches and schools because funds designated for Catholic education were stolen.[2]

- An employee of the American Diabetes Association embezzled nearly $570,000 from the Association. Instead of helping the 26 million Americans who have this disease, the stolen funds were spent at casinos, restaurants, and clothing stores.[3]
- A church treasurer who defrauded a Las Vegas church out of $1.75 million caused the church to lose their property to foreclosure.[4]

There are several ways to reduce the risk of fraud in your organization. Taking action before fraud occurs is certainly the wisest choice and would include proactive measures such as training or awareness campaigns and implementing internal control to increase accountability and transparency.

However, if you experience fraud at your organization, the actions you take will directly impact the risk of future fraud occurring. Taking reactive measures such as disciplinary action and fixing the process or controlling weaknesses can even be proactive. You are communicating to current and future employees that such behavior will not be tolerated.

TAKING DISCIPLINARY ACTION

While a major tenet of the church involves forgiveness, it is important to remember that fraud is a serious crime; the perpetrator has broken the law and breached a sacred trust. Richard Hammar, a legal expert in church and clergy issues, offers the following advice to church leaders when they find someone has committed a fraud:

- Find out how much money was actually taken. (Hire a local certified public accountant or certified fraud examiner, if necessary.)
- Require full restitution of the funds within a specified period of time.

- Have the embezzler sign a promissory note, detailing the amount to pay and the specified period of time.
- Permanently remove the embezzler from any position within the church that involves handling money.[5]

The question of whether to turn the case over to the police or local prosecutor is a question that each organization will have to answer for itself based on the circumstances of the case. This may also be necessary if the suspected embezzler doesn't confess or it isn't clear who is guilty.[6]

Whether or not to prosecute may also involve the severity of the fraud and the ability and willingness of the perpetrator to make restitution. As Hammar points out, since the embezzler probably didn't report the stolen funds as income, "in some cases it is more likely that the IRS will prosecute the embezzler for tax evasion than the local prosecutor will prosecute for the crime of embezzlement."[7]

Let me illustrate this consequence by elaborating on the outcomes of two of the stories that will be discussed later in this book.

A trusted volunteer was buying personal items at a local supermarket and charging those purchases to the church. After the volunteer was caught at the supermarket trying to make another fraudulent purchase, she was taken to the police station. The church decided not to prosecute if the volunteer made restitution. However, the volunteer was removed from her position and not allowed to volunteer for a period of time. She was repentant, and she made restitution over the next eighteen months. Although she was not allowed to hold any position in the church that involved handling money, she was restored to fellowship within the congregation. The woman and her husband remained active in the church for several years (pages 52–54).

The office manager of a nonprofit organization was caught using blank checks to make personal purchases for herself and her family. The organization initiated an internal investigation to determine the scope of her theft but didn't prosecute. In fact, they allowed the office manager to resign, instead of being fired, and didn't require restitution. She moved out of town and found another job as a bookkeeper at a church. While the church was checking her references, they called the previous employer for a recommendation and were only told that she resigned. Unfortunately for that church, the bookkeeper had no change of heart and was caught misusing funds again (pages 57–59).

These two stories highlight the different paths that organizations can take when they catch a trusted employee or volunteer stealing funds. In one case, the perpetrator was required to make restitution and went through a successful period of rehabilitation. In the other case, the perpetrator was allowed to resign and move on without any consequences, so she went on to repeat her self-serving and illegal behavior.

The dichotomy of these two outcomes would suggest that taking some sort of disciplinary action is more effective in stopping a person from continuing their abuse at another organization. However, not all organizations take significant disciplinary action.

According to the ACFE, 87 percent of occupational fraudsters have never been charged or convicted of fraud, and 82 percent have never been punished or fired for fraud-related conduct.[8] While this indicates that many fraudsters are first-time offenders, I believe it also indicates that employers do not always press charges against employees who steal. As a result, they are able to commit abuses at their next employer.

Nevertheless, statistics are somewhat encouraging for those

organizations that do take action. The ACFE study found that when an organization experienced fraud, 61 percent referred the case for criminal prosecution, while 22 percent filed a civil lawsuit instead of criminal action.[9] In those cases referred to law enforcement for criminal prosecution, 75 percent of the perpetrators pleaded guilty or were convicted.[10]

When a civil lawsuit was pursued, 82 percent received a judgment in favor of the organization or reached a settlement.[11] Unfortunately, while a majority received a favorable judgment, the ACFE research also indicates that 58 percent of organizations do not recover any of their losses.[12]

It's understandable that churches and nonprofits have a difficult time with a decision to prosecute or not. When organizations didn't refer a fraud case to law enforcement, the most often cited reason was the fear of bad publicity.[13]

Airing dirty laundry isn't a pleasant thought. It reveals your current processes are weak and allowed the abuse to occur. It may reveal that leaders weren't performing adequate oversight. It will let also donors know that their contributions didn't further the ministry of the organization but were used to line the pockets of someone they trusted.

Fear of bad publicity is a valid concern. Details of the scandal may be publicized on the front page of the local newspaper and may be the lead story on the evening news. Members may lose confidence in the ministry's ability to effectively perform their stated goals, and donors may move their funds elsewhere.

However, let me caution you that a decision not to take action may be just as harmful in the long run. In today's world of social media, instant communication, and constant connections, it is inevitable that news of the scandal will become known. While fear of bad publicity is normal, trying to hide bad news or "sweeping it under the rug" may be just as damaging. On the other hand, holding the perpetrator accountable will give opportunity for rehabilitation and protect unsuspecting organizations that may subsequently consider hiring that person.

CHAPTER FOUR

TOOLS TO REDUCE THE RISK OF FRAUD

THE POWER OF THE AUDIT

One way to ensure your processes, procedures, and controls are robust enough to prevent fraud from happening in your organization is to put them through the scrutiny of an audit. There are a few different types of audits that can be performed, from assessing the strength of your controls to considering whether your financial statements appear reasonable. Knowledgeable business people in your congregation or an independent public accounting firm can also perform these audits.

Before you decide on what type of audit you need or who will perform it, you should decide what your needs are. For example, do you need accurate financial statements to present to your board, congregation, or banking institution? Do you need to review your internal processes to assess compliance with your policies and procedures? Do you need to evaluate the effectiveness of a specific function in the church like payroll or accounts payable?

Additionally, consider your funding and resources. Do you have qualified business people within your congregation who are willing and available to perform a review? Do you have a trusted relationship with a local public accounting firm? Do you have available funding to pay for an in-depth audit?

Finally, you should review your constitution and bylaws. This document may have specific language regarding the type of audit required and how often it should be completed. Your bylaws may require audited financial statements annually, which would indicate an audit by a public accounting firm. However, if your bylaws require only a review of your finances on a regular basis, a review by qualified business people in the organization may suffice. Your specific needs will dictate the type of audit that should be performed.

A financial statement audit performed by an independent public accounting firm is called an external audit. The public accounting firm will ensure your organization's financial statements comply with generally accepted accounting principles (GAAP), and a certified public accountant (CPA) will express an opinion on whether those financial statements are relevant, complete, and fairly presented.

The focus of the public accounting firm is very specific. The accounting firm will focus on the presentation of the financial statements and compliance with GAAP. They will perform specific tests of internal controls and gather sufficient evidence on which to base their opinion. They will focus on material errors—those errors that will result in a misstatement of the financial statements and affect the decisions of informed readers of those financial statements.

A financial statement audit will evaluate your recordkeeping on the basis of rules and requirements designed to protect shareholders of public companies. When you chose this form of audit, your church is comparing your financial management reporting and processes to generally accepted accounting principles, an evaluation of external controls.

An internal audit may be more in line if your organization needs to focus on internal controls, operational effectiveness, and efficiency, or on ways to reduce risk. Qualified people within the organization can perform such an audit. Certainly, a local CPA firm can provide this same type of review, but significant cost savings can be gained by an internal audit performed by volunteers in the organization.

Some larger companies have an internal audit staff, whose function is to provide independent assurance and consulting services designed to improve an organization's operations. They can assist an organization in accomplishing its stated mission by evaluating the effectiveness of the organization's risk management, control, and governance process. The internal auditors also help detect and prevent fraud and ensure accurate financial reporting. While a church may not have a dedicated internal auditor on its staff, it probably has access to qualified business people in the congregation who are knowledgeable about corporate governance, accounting practices, and risk management.

If a financial statement audit isn't what your organization needs, a team of qualified people could be tasked to review your financial processes. Their objective would be to assess:

- The reliability and integrity of your financial information
- Compliance with internal policies and other laws and regulations
- Effectiveness and efficiency of operations

These types of reviews will address any errors that significantly impact the organization's ability to meet their stated goals and objectives.

AUDIT OPTIONS: WHICH ONE IS RIGHT FOR YOUR ORGANIZATION?

Review the following chart to determine which type of audit fits your situation.

External Audit

Process	Review of accounting practices and comparison to GAAP
Focus	Externally prepared financial statements that will be materially accurate
Benefit	Confidence in your accounting process and financial reporting

Internal Audit

Process   Review of financial operations and internal controls for strengths and weaknesses

Focus   Testing the accuracy of internally generated financial statements

Benefit   Confidence in your financial management process

PERFORMING A FRAUD RISK ASSESSMENT

As you read this book, you may be wondering if your financial practices are exposing your organization to the risk of fraud. One way to evaluate your risk is to perform a fraud risk assessment. I've included a tool to help you perform this assessment in Appendix A.

The assessment contains 56 questions designed to determine whether you have adequate controls in place to reduce the risk of fraud. Answer the questions honestly, and then score yourself using the instructions provided after the questionnaire. This tool will help you assess the strength or weakness of controls in key financial processes, including contributions and cash receipts, payments and disbursements, payroll, and financial reporting and reconciliation. This questionnaire will help you identify those controls that haven't been implemented or are not working as expected.

I encourage you to have a few of your leaders complete the assessment, including your bookkeeper and treasurer. Oftentimes, I find pastors and nonprofit leaders think their control processes are stronger than they actually are. By asking your frontline experts to complete the questionnaire, you may get a view of reality that you weren't expecting.

After you complete the assessment, follow the scoring instructions to evaluate your organization's fraud risk. You can evaluate your organization's overall control structure and then evaluate specific controls within five key processes. Once the assessment is completed and reviewed, you and your team can work on integrating those controls that you are lacking to increase accountability and transparency and reduce the risk of fraud.

PERFORMING AN INTERNAL AUDIT

As you consider the chart of audit options on pages 38–39, you may decide that an external audit by a CPA firm is not needed at this time. However, you may want to have a team of qualified business people review your financial operations and assess the adequacy of your processes and controls. I've included a tool in Appendix B that an internal audit team can use to perform this review.

The internal audit program in Appendix B is a step-by-step program that will help your internal audit team review the key processes in your organization where fraud and abuse usually occur—including cash and contribution processing, disbursements, credit cards, payroll, and fixed assets. Additionally, the audit team can review other areas that sometimes present problems for churches and nonprofits like IRS compliance and other governance issues.

The audit program gives specific tests for the team to perform and directs the team to review some of the more common processes and procedures where weaknesses often occur in churches and non-profits. This audit program is not meant to be exhaustive, and the audit team should review all areas and processes at your specific organization. For example, additional tests in inventory controls will be needed if the church has a coffee shop or bookstore. The fraud risk assessment in Appendix A is another tool that may help identify other areas where additional testing and review is needed—especially for those questions that could not be answered with a "yes."

After the team completes the audit program, the team can recommend improvements to the organization's processes based on any errors or weaknesses identified during the audit. I would encourage the audit team to document their results and provide a copy of their results to the leadership team and governing board. The board then will have a foundation to take appropriate action for safeguarding internal processes and procedures and protecting the organization from fraud.

The audit team should be empowered to follow up in three to six months to see if the recommended improvements have been implemented. The team may need to perform some tests from the initial audit again to evaluate the effectiveness of any new controls or processes. If the audit team discovers that some of the recommended improvements couldn't be implemented due to cost or available resources, the audit team should recommend alternative solutions to ensure control processes are strengthened and assets are protected. Further, I would encourage the audit team to perform a complete review of all processes on an annual basis.

I believe an internal audit is a beneficial tool to help reduce the risk of fraud in any organization. Certainly, an internal audit could uncover fraud or abuse occurring within the organization. As stated earlier, strong internal controls and other accountability measures (like internal audits) can help detect fraud sooner. As the ACFE study on fraud revealed, 30 percent of frauds were uncovered by management reviews and internal audits.[1] Additionally, knowing that in-depth review is being made and will occur regularly can also deter employees, volunteers, and members from future abuse.

EMBRACING ACCOUNTABILITY AND INTEGRITY

One of the most important steps leaders can take to prevent fraud from occurring in their church is to embrace accountability and integrity and decide these are nonnegotiable values in the church. This means practicing what you preach and modeling biblical stewardship.

While you and your leadership are modeling these nonnegotiable values, weave these themes into your preaching and teaching. Teach on stewardship regularly and the importance of accountability and integrity in personal finances as well as corporate finance. Be transparent by providing regular financial reports.

The Evangelical Council for Financial Accountability is an organization dedicated to improving the public's trust in Christian ministries.[2] It has established the "Seven Standards of Responsible Stewardship," which focus on board governance, financial transparency, integrity in fund-raising, and proper use of charity resources.

I would encourage your ministry to review and adopt these stewardship standards to demonstrate your commitment to biblical stewardship and financial accountability. For more information about the ECFA and their stewardship standards, visit their website at http://www.ECFA.org.

ECFA's Seven Standards of Responsible Stewardship

Standard 1 — Doctrinal Issues: Every organization shall subscribe to a written statement of faith clearly affirming a commitment to the evangelical Christian faith or shall otherwise demonstrate such commitment, and shall operate in accordance with biblical truths and practices.

Standard 2 — Governance: Every organization shall be governed by a responsible board of not less than five individuals, a majority of whom shall be independent, who shall meet at least semiannually to establish policy and review its accomplishments.

Standard 3 — Financial Oversight: Each organization shall prepare complete and accurate financial statements. The board or a committee consisting of a majority of independent members shall approve the engagement of an independent certified public accountant, review the annual financial statements, and maintain appropriate communication with the independent certified public accountant. The board shall be apprised of any material weaknesses in internal control or other significant risks.

Standard 4 — Use of Resources and Compliance with Laws: Every organization shall exercise the appropriate management and controls necessary to provide reasonable assurance that all of the organization's operations are carried out and resources are used in a responsible manner and in conformity with applicable laws and regulations, such conformity taking into account biblical mandates.

Standard 5 — Transparency: Every organization shall provide a copy of its current financial statements upon written request and shall provide other disclosures as the law may require. The financial statements required to comply with Standard 3 must be disclosed under this standard.

An organization must provide a report, upon written request, including financial information on any specific project for which it has sought or is seeking gifts.

Standard 6 — Compensation-Setting and Related-Party Transactions: Every organization shall set compensation of its top leader and address related-party transactions in a manner that demonstrates integrity and propriety in conformity with ECFA's Policy for Excellence in Compensation-Setting and Related-Party Transactions.

Standard 7 — Stewardship of Charitable Gifts:

7.1 Truthfulness in Communications: In securing charitable gifts, all representations of fact, descriptions of the financial condition of the organization, or narratives about events must be current, complete, and accurate. References to past activities or events must be appropriately dated. There must be no material omissions or exaggerations of fact, use of misleading photographs or any other communication which would tend to create a false impression or misunderstanding.

7.2 Giver Expectations and Intent: Statements made about the use of gifts by an organization in its charitable gift appeals must be honored. A giver's intent relates both to what was communicated in the appeal and to any instructions accompanying the gift, if accepted by the organization. Appeals for charitable gifts must not create unrealistic expectations of what a gift will actually accomplish.

7.3 Charitable Gift Communication: Every organization shall provide givers appropriate and timely gift acknowledgments.

7.4 Acting in the Best Interest of Givers: When dealing with persons regarding commitments on major gifts, an organization's representatives must seek to guide and advise givers to adequately consider their broad interests.

An organization must make every effort to avoid knowingly accepting a gift from or entering into a contract with a giver that would place a hardship on the giver or place the giver's future well-being in jeopardy.

7.5 Percentage Compensation for Securing Charitable Gifts: An organization may not base compensation of outside stewardship resource consultants or its own employees directly or indirectly on a percentage of charitable contributions raised.

CASE STUDIES

*True Stories of Fraud and
Practical Ways to Prevent It*

SKIMMING DONATIONS

THE DIRECTOR had finished unpacking the last moving box when the bookkeeper walked into his office. "I have a confession," she said quietly. The director sat down and listened as the bookkeeper confessed to skimming donations received through the ministry's mail.

The director had been selected recently to lead the ministry that was dedicated to helping orphans, foster kids, and teenage mothers. He had introduced himself to each staff member and scheduled his first staff meeting. The bookkeeper's sudden confession surprised him, but it also puzzled him. "Why confess now?" he thought to himself.

He soon had his answer. The bookkeeper stated that she didn't want to continue her deceit any longer. She wanted the organization and the new director to succeed and offered her resignation.

She went on to explain how she had committed her abuse. The organization often solicited donations in the forms of cash and gift cards. Both were used to provide personal items for the children that the ministry supported.

She explained that whenever the secretary received cash in the mail, the cash was counted by two people and recorded in a log. The cash and a copy of the log were provided to the bookkeeper, who made the deposit and recorded the contribution.

Any gift cards received in the mail, however, were given directly to the bookkeeper. The team members who counted the cash did not count or make a record of the gifts cards received.

The bookkeeper maintained a log of the gift cards, but she didn't list each gift card individually, only a total of the gift cards by vendor. For example, if five Wal-Mart gift cards for $20 were received in May, she would list that as "$100 to Wal-Mart" in her spreadsheet.

When the bookkeeper received an approved purchase request, she would determine if there was an appropriate gift card that could be used for the purchase. If so, she would give the gift card to the staff member who would make the purchase and then return the gift card with the receipt. The bookkeeper would log the purchase in her spreadsheet and code it to the correct expense account. She tried to mark the remaining balance on each gift card, but that didn't always happen.

At the end of each month, she would forward the gift card spreadsheets to the local accounting firm, which would record the total gift cards received as revenue (donation in kind) and post the gift card usage to the correct expense accounts.

The bookkeeper admitted that she didn't always record all the gift cards in her spreadsheets. At various times over the years, she would take various gift cards and use them to make personal purchases, but she wasn't sure how much she had taken.

The ministry director suspended the bookkeeper and immediately began an investigation.

According to the financial records, the organization received between $14,000 and $16,000 in donated gift cards each year. In the past five years, the organization received about $76,800. During the same period, the bookkeeper had recorded that $69,500 in gift cards had been used to support children associated with the ministry.

Unfortunately, an audit revealed that there was no way to verify the accuracy of the bookkeeper's spreadsheets. It was apparent some records were incomplete or missing. Therefore, the auditor couldn't substantiate the total amount of gift cards received and used. This also made it difficult to determine how many gift cards were taken from the ministry and converted for personal use.

The auditor found 462 gift cards throughout the bookkeeper's office. They were not locked up or secured in any container. Some were in her desk drawer, some were on top of the desk, some were in a box on her credenza, and some were inside her credenza. The gift cards ranged from six cents to $100 each. There were approximately 25 different vendors representing clothing stores, grocery stores, bookstores, electronics showrooms, and office suppliers, as well as prepaid Visa cards.

Although the auditor expected that these gift cards would total an unused value of $7,300 (gift cards received less gift cards used), the organization would have to call the vendor on all 462 gift cards to know for sure.

Unfortunately, too many weaknesses existed within this organization to determine the total value of gift cards misused, whether other employees were involved, and whether the value of gift cards received and used were accurately reported on the organization's financial records.

After the investigation, the employee was fired but did offer to make restitution of a specified amount in lieu of prosecution.

WHAT WENT WRONG

In this case study, abuse occurred because there was a lack of accountability for gift cards received in the mail. Unfortunately, the person who opened the mail just delivered the gift cards to the bookkeeper without documenting the amounts received. The bookkeeper was the only person recording receipt and use of gift cards. A second person was not made responsible for reconciling the gift card usage and ensuring the amounts recorded in the financial records were accurate.

Additionally, poor controls existed over the custody of the gift cards. The gift cards were not stored in a secure cabinet. Not only did the bookkeeper have unrestricted access to the gift cards, but other employees could have walked into the office and taken gift cards for their own personal use too.

Further, the ministry did not send contribution receipts to donors for their gift card donations, meaning significant contributions were not acknowledged by the ministry. If receipts or acknowledgment letters had been sent, a second person could have used those letters to verify the accuracy of the gift card logs.

BEST PRACTICES

Churches and other ministries currently receive most of their income through cash donations. Donations of cash and checks are collected during worship services or mailed to the church office.

While cash donations are more frequent, gift cards can be a convenient way for donors to make contributions to certain ministries. However, gift cards are easily convertible to cash and must be safeguarded just like cash.

Skimming is a type of fraud scheme where cash is stolen from an organization before it can be recorded in the financial records. If proper controls are not in place, skimming is a fraud risk that all churches face. Cash can be skimmed from the offering plate, from the mail, from the bookstore, or from the coffee shop—anywhere a church might receive cash.

Skimming is one of the more frequent ways funds are stolen from an organization, but can be difficult to identify. According to the ACFE study, skimming occurred in 12.5 percent of fraud cases at religious and charitable organizations, and skimming fraud often lasted eighteen months before being discovered.[1]

For this reason, churches need to have strong controls over cash receipts and donations. For example, all cash and gift card donations must be received, counted, and logged by at least two people. The gift card logs should reflect the original amount of the donation and any use of the card. The remaining balances on the gift cards should be reconciled by someone other than the custodian of the gift cards, and the gift cards must be stored in a secure cabinet or container.

Further, contribution receipts should be sent to the donors to acknowledge their gifts. This process will also provide secondary accountability by helping to find any discrepancies between the actual and reported gift card amounts.

EVALUATE YOUR ORGANIZATION

- Are all incoming cash and gift cards received, counted, and logged by at least two people? Who are they? What functions do they perform?
- Are cash and gift cards properly safeguarded while in your custody? Where are they stored? Who has access? How secure is the actual storage location?
- Is gift card usage reported accurately in the financial records?
- Are receipts sent to donors for gift card contributions and copies maintained in the files?
- Are gift card logs (received and used) reconciled by someone other than the gift card custodian? Who performs the reconciliation? How often? How are differences resolved?

FOR FURTHER REVIEW

Would you like to know if your controls are strong enough to prevent skimming from happening at your ministry? Review the internal audit program in Appendix B, and perform a mini-audit by completing the audit steps in the Contributions and Cash Receipts section. Consider changes to policy or process to strengthen controls over cash and in-kind donations if any weaknesses exist.

SECRET BANK ACCOUNT

URING the monthly meeting to review the ministry's financial operations, the bookkeeper went through the details of revenue and expenses, upcoming bills, and available cash. The ministry director was particularly interested in the funds collected to help open a campus ministry in the area. The bookkeeper reminded him that all funds collected were deposited into a separate bank account segregated from other ministry funds. She stated that although the campus ministry had recently opened, few funds remained left to be disbursed; and after paying a few outstanding invoices, the campus ministry fund would be depleted.

The ministry director was satisfied with the information and directed the bookkeeper to pay the remaining bills and then close the campus ministry bank account.

The bookkeeper paid the remaining bills but kept the bank account open until the final few checks had cleared the account. During the next monthly meeting, the bookkeeper stated that the final bills were paid, and the bank account would be closed soon, as a few checks still had not cleared the bank. She explained it would take another month for the final checks to process through the account. The ministry director smiled and crossed the item off the agenda. "I guess we can remove this from the agenda," he stated. And with the strike of a pen, the topic of the campus ministry bank account was never revisited.

Unfortunately, the bookkeeper didn't close the campus ministry bank account, soon realizing that she was the only one who knew the account was still open. Since she was the person who opened the mail, including the bank statements, she was able to conceal the fact that the account was still open.

The bookkeeper began transferring money from the operating fund to the campus ministry fund. She started small — transferring only a few hundred dollars, disguising the transfer in the financial records as a routine expense.

Even though she was confident that no one would notice the transfer, she waited. As the organization's bookkeeper, she was an authorized signer on the bank accounts, which allowed her to write checks, make transfers, and withdraw funds. No one, not even the ministry director, looked at the financial records in detail, choosing only to see summary reports.

After a few weeks passed, no one had asked about the transfer, so the bookkeeper went to the bank and withdrew the money.

The next month, the bookkeeper decided it was time for another transfer. Only this time, the transfer was a little larger. Again, she concealed the transfer as a routine expense, and she went to the bank and made a withdrawal. Over the next year, she continued to make large transfers from the operating fund into the campus ministry fund. After each transfer, she went to the bank and withdrew all the funds.

Fortunately, while no one at the nonprofit noticed the embezzlement, someone at the bank was taking notice. The alert bank employee began noticing a pattern — after each transfer into the account, the bookkeeper would withdraw all the funds. The suspicious pattern caused the bank manager to contact the ministry director.

By the time the ministry director learned about the scheme, the bookkeeper had embezzled more than $57,600 over two years. After a short investigation, the bookkeeper was terminated and agreed to make restitution in lieu of criminal prosecution.

WHAT WENT WRONG

In this case study, the bookkeeper was entrusted to close an unneeded bank account. Certainly, most employees in our churches and ministries are trustworthy. However, abuse can occur when a lack of accountability exists. In this case study, no one followed up to make sure the bookkeeper actually closed the account. As a result, the bookkeeper was able to keep the second bank account hidden, transfer funds into the secret account, and use the funds for personal expenses.

Several internal control weaknesses allowed this abuse to occur, including:

- The organization's management failed to review the book-keeper's actions to ensure the bank account was closed.

- The bookkeeper had signature authority for all bank accounts and the ability to transfer funds without additional approval.

- The bookkeeper received all the mail, including the bank statements.

As a result of these weaknesses, the bookkeeper had complete control over the financial records. This allowed the bookkeeper to disguise her transactions, manipulate reports, and conceal her fraudulent activity.

BEST PRACTICES

Segregation of duties is an important internal control. No one employee should have unrestricted and unaccountable control over the finances. In many churches and ministries, the accounting function is limited to one or two people. As a result, one person usually has total control over the finances. However, additional measures can be added to provide accountability and oversight.

As noted earlier (page 25), the survey completed by KPMG in 2011 found 74 percent of fraudsters were able to perpetrate their crimes by exploiting weak internal controls.[1] This was a significant increase from their 2007 study that found only 49 percent of fraud cases occurred by exploiting weak controls.[2]

A lack of accountability is a common weakness in nonprofit organizations, which can lead to significant abuse. For example, in August 2013, the CEO of a nonprofit charter school in Philadelphia pled guilty to stealing $88,000. Through bank accounts that only he controlled, the CEO withdrew funds from the school and a sister organization, a portion of which he used to purchase a house for himself. He concealed his activity by disguising the withdrawals as legitimate labor expenses.[3]

While industry experts and best practices encourage accountability and strong controls, this continues to be the weak link in the financial processes at many churches and nonprofits. In order to keep all bank activity accountable and transparent in your organization, consider implementing these controls:

- Limit signature authority on bank accounts to those who are needed to transact business.

- Separate the functions of writing checks and reconciling bank activity.

- Ensure that the person who reconciles the bank account receives all bank statements.

- Require proper approval for all checks, electronic fund transfers, withdrawals, and wire transfers before the transaction occurs.

EVALUATE YOUR ORGANIZATION

- Do you limit signature authority on bank accounts to those who are needed to transact business? Who currently has signature authority? What functions do they perform?

- Do you separate the functions of writing checks from the bank reconciliation activity? Who performs each of these functions?

- Do all bank statements go directly to the person who reconciles the bank account? Are there any exceptions to this process? How often and why?

- Do all checks, electronic fund transfers, withdrawals, and wire transfers require proper approval before the transaction occurs? What is the approval process and who is involved?

FOR FURTHER REVIEW

Would you like to know if your controls are strong enough to prevent abuse of separate accounts from happening at your ministry? Review the internal audit program in Appendix B, and perform a mini-audit by completing the audit steps in the Bank Activity and Reconciliations section. Consider changes to policy or process to strengthen account recordkeeping and review if any weaknesses exist.

WRITING BLANK CHECKS

THE PRESIDENT of the organization sat at his desk, stunned. An independent auditor had just walked into his office and revealed that a trusted employee was probably stealing funds from the ministry. Even more disturbing was that the theft had been occurring for at least eighteen months. Several questions raced through the president's mind: "Is this true?" "How could this happen?" "Why didn't we catch this earlier?" "How are we going to move forward?"

ABC Publishing[1] was a ministry organization that printed religious materials, training resources, and Bibles in various languages. Their staff included missionaries, editors, and translators. Many staff and department leaders often traveled overseas to track the progress of their ongoing projects, leaving the small administrative and support staff alone in the office.

The office manager was assigned the task of overseeing much of the office's administrative duties, including purchasing office supplies, office décor, and hospitality items. When the office manager needed to make a purchase, she would submit a purchase request to the vice-president for approval. Upon approval, the chief financial officer (CFO) would write a check and have an authorized person sign the check. Only the president, vice-president, and chief financial officer were authorized to sign checks. If an invoice wasn't attached to the purchase request, the CFO asked the office manager to return the check stub with an invoice or receipt once the purchase was made.

Often, the exact total of the purchase wasn't known when the purchase request was submitted. The vendor's name and a description of the items being purchased were on the request, but not a total dollar amount. The organizational leadership agreed to sign a blank check as long as the office manager turned in a receipt afterwards.

The first time the office manager requested a blank check to purchase office supplies, the CFO requested she bring back the check stub and receipt. After making the purchase, she carefully folded the receipt so the purchase total was clearly visible and stapled it to the check stub. When she returned the check stub to the CFO, he asked her two questions: "Did the vice-president approve this purchase?" and "Did you attach the receipt to the check stub?" The office manager answered yes to both questions, knowing that the exchange was just a formality since the CFO had the vice-president sign the blank check and he could see that the receipt was attached to the check stub.

The office manager watched as the CFO went to his computer, opened the financial software program, entered the check into the financial records, and placed the check stub in the filing cabinet with paperwork for other completed transactions.

She walked away and thought, "That worked well." Over the next few weeks, she requested a couple more blank checks. After a while, she realized that while the CFO would always ask the two standard questions, he never actually looked at the receipt. Further, the vice-president never asked to review the receipt before she returned it to the CFO. The office manager appreciated the fact that the organization's leadership viewed her as a trusted employee, but she also realized she had more freedom than she had previously thought.

The president shook his head in disbelief and asked the auditor to explain what had happened. As far as the auditor could tell, at some point, the office manager realized that even though she turned in a receipt for every blank check, no one actually reviewed the receipt to make sure the items purchased were business-related. While the auditor didn't know the reason behind the office manager's actions, it was evident that she soon realized she could make personal purchases and use ministry funds to pay for it.

When the auditor reviewed the receipts as part of his normal testing, he discovered that gift cards were included in many of these transactions that started with a blank check. The gift cards, which could be purchased near the checkout lane, were clearly identified on the receipts and included restaurant, grocery, and retail establishments. As he looked through the financial files, he determined that these gift card purchases had started approximately eighteen months earlier. At first, the gift card amounts were low, but over time, the auditor noticed that the gift card amounts increased. He also noticed that several gift cards were purchased at a time—each one clearly itemized on the receipt.

The auditor noticed that while the office manager had turned in the receipts, she was clearly trying to hide her activity. In fact, she purposely folded the receipt and stapled it in such a way to hide the items being purchased. Someone would have to remove the staple and unfold the receipt in order to view the list of purchased items.

The organization's president confirmed to the auditor that his organization didn't use or give away gift cards. These gift cards were definitely unapproved purchases. The president confronted the employee and suspended her. The case was then turned over to legal counsel for further review and investigation.

By the time the auditor uncovered the theft, the office manager had purchased $9,000 in gift cards, ranging in amounts from $25 to $300.

WHAT WENT WRONG

In this case study, the office manager was a very talented and trusted employee. Due to her length of time at the organization, her passion for the ministry, and her accomplishments in the past, she had the trust and confidence of her supervisors.

As a result, her supervisors didn't give a second thought to handing her a blank check.

While the CFO provided a measure of accountability by writing the vendor's name on the check, the office manager's only required task was to write the amount on the check at the store checkout. However, she abused her supervisor's trust by adding personal items to the purchase and using ministry funds for payment.

Several internal control weaknesses allowed this abuse to occur, which included:

- The office manager submitted her purchase for preapproval, but no manager reviewed her purchases afterward.
- The vice-president frequently signed blank checks for the office manager's use.
- The office manager's purchases were not reviewed to determine if the items purchased complied with internal policies.
- The president, vice-president, and CFO all failed to hold the office manager accountable for her purchases.

BEST PRACTICES

Writing blank checks is a fast and convenient way to allow employees to make purchases. However, signed blank checks can be easily abused. Not only can the checks be written for more than the approved amounts, but also they can be used for entirely different purchases.

Issuing unauthorized checks or "check tampering" is a common fraud scheme. For example, in April 2013, an office manager was sentenced to almost three years in prison for embezzling more than $900,000 from her employer using this scheme. She was able to convince the check signers at the company to sign blank checks under the assumption that they would be used to pay company expenses. Instead, she cashed the checks and used the money for her own personal benefit. Once the blank checks were signed, she tried to conceal the fraud and implicate someone else by making the checks out to another employee and then forging the employee's endorsement on the back of the check. Besides the fraud, she was also convicted of identity theft.[2]

One recent fraud study found issuing or forging unauthorized company checks was the most common embezzlement scheme.[3] Another study found that check tampering was the most common fraud scheme perpetrated at religious and charitable organizations.[4] Unfortunately, the median duration of check tampering schemes lasted around twenty-six months before being discovered.[5]

Don't let this happen at your organization. When writing checks, there are several steps a church can take to keep fraud from occurring. These controls include:

- Maintaining a policy to never sign blank checks
- Securing blank check stock in a locked cabinet
- Keeping track of check numbers used and reconciling check numbers to remaining blank check stock
- Matching supporting documents to each check's amount before signing checks
- Requiring supporting documents to be original invoices or receipts—not copies, partial documents, or estimates
- Using purchase requests or requisition forms to authorize purchases before they occur
- Reviewing itemized receipts or invoices for appropriateness and compliance with the organization's policies

EVALUATE YOUR ORGANIZATION

- Do you make it a practice to never sign blank checks? Do exceptions occur? Why?

- Do you secure blank check stock in a locking cabinet? Who has access to the locking cabinet?

- Do you keep track of prenumbered check stock and reconcile unused check numbers to the checks already printed? Who performs this reconciliation? How often?

- Do you review supporting documents and match amounts to the checks before signing? Who performs this review? What happens if supporting documents aren't available?

- Do you require original invoices and receipts for payment? What happens if original documents aren't available?

- Do you require properly approved purchase requests or requisition forms before purchases are made? What is the process to get approval? Who has authority to approve purchases?

- Do you review the itemized receipts or invoices for appropriateness and compliance with the organization's policies? Who performs this review? What happens if a purchase doesn't comply with policy?

FOR FURTHER REVIEW

Would you like to know if your controls are strong enough to prevent check tampering from happening at your ministry? Review the internal audit program in Appendix B, and perform a mini-audit by completing the audit steps in the *Cash Disbursements and Purchasing* section. Consider changes to policy or process to strengthen accountability and review of purchases if any weaknesses exist.

CHARGE ACCOUNTS

THE CHURCH bookkeeper ended the conversation by stating, "I'll be right there," and hung up the phone. His wife could see the look of disbelief on his face and asked him what was going on. "That was the police," he began. "They just arrested the hospitality coordinator. I have to go to the police station."

Main Street Church had been in the community for more than fifty years. Family members of the founding group that started the congregation still attended each week. The church had grown large enough that they needed a person to oversee the hospitality ministry. This person was assigned to manage the kitchen, order supplies and food, and organize the meals for special dinners, funerals, or church functions.

In order to facilitate her purchasing requests, the church opened up a revolving charge account with a local supermarket. The supermarket provided personalized cards that would allow the bearer to charge the purchase to the church. The church provided these cards to several people, including the hospitality coordinator.

Each month, the supermarket would send a bill to the church with a summary of the charges. In order to properly code the expenses, the bookkeeper requested each person who used the supermarket charge card to turn in the receipts. At the end of the month, the bookkeeper would match the receipts to the monthly bill, allocate the purchases to the appropriate expense account, and pay the bill.

Unfortunately, the bookkeeper realized that several receipts were missing each month. He was obligated to pay the bill, but he didn't know how to allocate several purchases each month. He was also unsure of whether it was an appropriate purchase, or if the supermarket had charged the church's account improperly.

The bookkeeper met with each person who had a supermarket charge card. He reminded them that they must turn in the receipts each time they used the card and showed them the few purchases each month that were unaccounted for. Unfortunately, each person denied making the mysterious purchases.

The bookkeeper considered keeping the charge cards locked up and under the supervision of the office manager. The office manager could hand out the cards when needed and retrieve them after the purchase was completed. When the card was returned, she could make sure that the receipt was turned in with it. However, this additional control was met with resistance from church leaders. The office manager worked part time, and none of the employees wanted to be restricted to shopping only when the office manager was working.

The bookkeeper had two more months go by without any improvement in the number of receipts being turned in. He realized if he couldn't get his staff's support, maybe he could get the supermarket's support. He met with the supermarket's accounting department, who agreed to send copies of the receipts with each month's bill. At last, the bookkeeper would have all matching receipts and be able to allocate the expenses to the appropriate department.

When he opened up the next month's bill, the bookkeeper was shocked at what he saw. All the receipts were included, but he didn't expect to see some of the items that were purchased. Included with some of the purchases were several supermarket gift cards. These gift cards, which could only be used at this supermarket, ranged in value from $50 to $200. He considered that these may have been purchased to give to a needy family, but a quick conversation with the pastor revealed that wasn't the case.

He wondered if this may have been the reason that past receipts hadn't been turned it. He contacted the supermarket manager, who was able to provide receipts for the previous twelve months. As he feared, the receipts that had been missing all included gift cards in the purchase.

The bookkeeper still didn't know who was doing this, so he interviewed the staff one more time with the new information. Again, each person denied making the purchases that included the gift cards.

The bookkeeper asked for the supermarket's help again. He asked them to require signatures when the charge card was used. When the next month's bill arrived, there were signatures on each receipt. However, he was shocked to see several receipts still included gift cards—and flabbergasted to see the name of the pastor's wife scrawled on the bottom of those receipts.

Fortunately, the bookkeeper had known the pastor's wife long enough to recognize her signature, and this was clearly a forgery. Someone had been stealing from the church—someone willing to implicate the pastor's wife.

The bookkeeper visited with the supermarket management team one more time. Along with the questionable receipts, he carried the most recent pictorial directory of the church. All staff members who had used a church charge card had their pictures in this directory.

The supermarket's management team was clearly concerned. Not only did the church have poor controls over their purchasing process, but the supermarket had some poor controls too. The supermarket staff had allowed someone to fraudulently charge purchases to the church.

Thankfully, the receipts listed the ID of the cashier and time of day. Management talked with the cashier, who recalled the most recent transaction. They asked her to look through the directory and pick out the church member who came through her line that day. It didn't take her long to find the picture. She pointed to the picture of the hospitality coordinator and exclaimed, "That's her!"

Incredibly, the hospitality coordinator went back to the supermarket to make another purchase. But this time, the supermarket staff was on the lookout. As soon as she entered the store, they called the police. Before she could check out, she was arrested.

By the time the scheme was discovered, the bookkeeper estimated the hospitality coordinator had purchased over $4,000 in personal items and shopping cards.

WHAT WENT WRONG

In this case study, a trusted leader in the church had abused the church's charge account at a local supermarket. Unfortunately, trust is not an effective internal control.

Several weaknesses allowed this abuse to occur, including:

- Staff members were allowed to charge purchases to the church account without any preapproval.

- There wasn't an effective process to make sure staff members turned in receipts after a purchase was charged to the church account.

- There was a lack of accountability to ensure that purchases were appropriate and complied with the church's policies.

Not only did the church have poor procedures, but so did the supermarket. The supermarket was complicit in this scheme because it allowed people to charge purchases to the church account without verifying who they were.

BEST PRACTICES

Having a charge account at a local supermarket or wholesale food store is a convenient way to make purchases. Several employees can be authorized to make purchases for the church, the employees don't have to request a church check for the purchase, and the church only receives one bill at the end of the month.

However, these benefits are also the reason charge accounts can be abused. Employees can make purchases without first obtaining authorization, employees can bypass any accountability measures by not turning in receipts, and churches can lose visibility of purchase totals until the monthly bill arrives.

In order to keep charge account purchases accountable, consider implementing these controls:

- Restrict access to charge accounts to as few employees as possible.
- Use purchase request forms to authorize any charge account activity before it occurs.
- Request the store to require proper identification and signatures for each charge purchase.
- Require employees to turn in receipts after each purchase.
- Reconcile receipts to the monthly bill.
- Review itemized receipts for appropriateness and compliance with the organization's policies.

As an additional measure of control, consider keeping the charge cards locked up. The charge card could be handed out once the purchase is authorized, and the purchaser would be required to return the receipt with the card once the purchase has been completed.

EVALUATE YOUR ORGANIZATION

- Do you restrict access to charge accounts to only those employees who have a valid need? Who are those employees? What functions do they perform?

- Do you use purchase request forms to authorize any charge account activity before it occurs? Who authorizes purchases on charge accounts?

- Do you require the store to check for proper identification and obtain a signature for each charge purchase?

- Do you require employees to turn in receipts after each purchase? What happens if receipts are not turned in?

- Do you reconcile receipts to the monthly bill? What happens if discrepancies are noted?

- Do you review the itemized receipts for appropriateness and compliance with the organization's policies? What happens if a purchase doesn't comply with policy?

- Do you have an adequate process to keep track of the charge cards and obtain all receipts? Is there anything you can do to strengthen the process?

FOR FURTHER REVIEW

Would you like to know if your controls are strong enough to prevent charge account abuse from happening at your ministry? Review the internal audit program in Appendix B, and perform a mini-audit by completing the audit steps in the Credit Card and Charge Accounts section. Consider changes to policy or process to strengthen oversight of these accounts if any weaknesses exist.

SEPARATE CHECKING ACCOUNTS

THE BOARD MEMBER'S question made the senior pastor pause for a moment. As he reflected on the question, he wasn't sure why the youth pastor had a checking account separate from the church's main checking account.

He remembered it was that way when he became senior pastor fifteen years earlier. Although this current youth pastor had only been here for a few years, the senior pastor allowed the separate finances to continue. "If it worked before, why change it?" he remembered thinking.

He quickly thought through the process. The youth pastor set his own budget each year, raised his own funds, purchased any ministry items and supplies, and reported on his ministry's financial operations each year at the annual business meeting.

While the youth minister's salary and benefits were paid through the church's general fund, most everything else related to the youth ministry was run through the youth checking account. At times, the church board would transfer funds to the youth ministry for a special project or need, but it was only occasionally.

But now, some of the board member's concerns seemed to make sense. Any offerings collected during the youth service were handled by the youth pastor or his youth workers. The senior pastor assumed that the youth ministry had good procedures to count the offerings, but he couldn't be sure. Further, he didn't know how youth funds were actually spent, or what they were spent on, other than the summary report he saw once a year with everyone else at the annual business meeting. He thought the youth pastor mentioned that he used financial software to help manage the ministry finances, but he wasn't sure which one.

After discussing the potential risks that could occur when one person has complete control over contributions, disbursements, and reporting, he agreed that it was appropriate to have the youth ministry fund combined with the rest of the church's finances. The two also discussed that this decision would involve several changes. Two ushers would have to collect the youth offering and place it in the church safe so that it could be counted with the other church offerings. The youth's income and expense activity for the current year would have to be combined with all the other church financial activity so that monthly and annual reports would be complete. The youth minister would no longer have authority to write checks. The youth checking account would need to be closed, and any remaining funds would be transferred to the church's main checking account. The youth minister would have to submit check requests for review and approval, and all checks would have to be signed by two board members.

While the change could be overwhelming to the youth minister, the senior pastor realized it would bring all ministry leaders in the church under the same financial process and accountability.

The pastor presented the idea to the board, who agreed with the decision. When the change was presented to the youth minister, he seemed to embrace the new process and accountability. Immediately, youth offerings were collected and counted with the main church offerings. The youth minister began submitting check requests for review and approval, and two board members signed the checks.

However, the youth minister didn't turn over his checkbook register, detailed financial reports for the past year, or even a backup of his financial software. At first, he needed time to enter recent activity into the financial software. Then he needed time to reconcile the bank statements. Subsequently, his hard drive got corrupted, and he needed to reinstall all of his software and recreate data. However, he said he didn't back up his financial data, so he would have to reenter all the financial activity for the past year.

These excuses kept occurring for several months, which made the pastor and board suspicious. Since they weren't getting any cooperation from the youth minister, the pastor went to the bank for help. The bank provided bank statements and copies of all canceled checks for the past two years. When the pastor and treasurer reviewed the activity, they understood why the youth minister had been unwilling to provide his financial activity.

A review of the bank activity revealed that the youth minister was using ministry funds for expenses that were not allowed or appropriate. While no other staff member's spouse had a cell phone paid for by the church, the youth minister felt it was appropriate for his wife to have a cell phone paid for with youth funds. While church policy allowed occasional business lunches, the youth minister used ministry funds to purchase frequent lunches. He also used ministry funds to purchase snack food and nutrition bars that he kept in his office. Further, the pastor noticed that when some of his requests for equipment purchases were not approved by the board, the youth minster used youth funds to make the purchase.

It was apparent that when the youth minister had the freedom to make his own purchase decisions, he frequently used ministry funds for purchases that were not appropriate or allowed under church policy.

WHAT WENT WRONG

In this case study, a ministry leader was able to collect offerings, make deposits, and spend funds without submitting his activity to any other review or approval. Several control weaknesses allowed this abuse to occur, including:

- The youth minister was allowed to have a separate checking account that was not included with or rolled into the church's financial records.
- The youth minister's financial activity was not reviewed or approved by another ministry leader.
- The youth minister did not have a clear understanding of what expenses were appropriate for his ministry.

Additionally, the church did not have clear policies on how ministry funds should be managed. One of the easiest, and most important, protections a church can implement is the documentation of formal accounting policies and procedures, personnel policies, and other operating policies.

BEST PRACTICES

Most churches will have a small bookkeeping staff that oversees the financial processes. All transactions will run through this process, including contributions and expenses. However, some ministry leaders may see the centralized process as burdensome, stifling, and restrictive. These ministry leaders may request to separate their ministry funds to streamline processes. This is how the youth minister in this case study was able to justify having a separate checking account.

However, the risks of having separate financial processes and bank accounts outweighed the benefits in this case. The youth minister was able to make purchases that were not accountable to anyone else, resulting in abuse.

In order to keep all financial activity accountable and transparent, consider implementing these controls:

- Require all offerings and contributions to follow the same collection, counting, and deposit process.
- Do not allow ministry leaders to have separate bank accounts.

- Require all expenditures to follow the same request and approval process.

- Review purchases for appropriateness and compliance with church's policies.

- Prepare consolidated financial reports that include income and expenses for all departments.

Finally, remember that documented policies and procedures are an important component of strong internal controls. Written policies and procedures will provide accountability for staff members, define expectations, and minimize confusion.

EVALUATE YOUR ORGANIZATION

- Do you require all offerings and contributions to follow the same collection, counting, and deposit process? Are there any exceptions? Why?

- Do you allow ministry leaders to have separate bank accounts? Who are they? Why?

- Do you require all expenditures to follow the same request and approval process? Are there any exceptions? Why?

- Do you hold employees accountable by reviewing purchases for appropriateness and compliance with church's policies? Who performs this review? What happens if a purchase doesn't comply with policy?

- Do you prepare consolidated financial reports that include income and expenses for all departments? If not, why not? Are other reports available?

- Are your accounting policies and procedures, personnel policies, and other operating policies documented? Who has access to these documented policies? Have all appropriate personnel read and understood these documented policies?

FOR FURTHER REVIEW

Would you like to know if your controls are strong enough to prevent misappropriation of funds from happening at your ministry? Review the internal audit program in Appendix B, and perform a mini-audit by completing the audit steps in the Cash Disbursements and Purchasing section. Consider changes to policy or process to purchasing controls if any weaknesses exist.

ELECTRONIC FUND TRANSFERS

THE INTERIM PASTOR sat down at his desk, opened the mail, and scanned the monthly statement for fuel charges. As the vendor intended, the bright red "past due" notice caught his eye. He had only been interim pastor for twenty days, but he didn't recognize this charge account. He was prepared to find a few bills that might have been overlooked during the transition, but as he reviewed the church's financial files, he didn't see any past activity for this particular company.

"This must be a mistake," he thought to himself. He set the bill aside and made a mental note to have the secretary call the company and have them correct their mistake.

The next day, the pastor received another confusing bill in the mail. This time, the bill was from a local wholesale club, and the balance due was significant. A quick scan of the monthly statement determined that a majority of the balance had been carried over from the previous month. Only a small payment had been made in the past thirty days to fulfill the minimum payment due. Because the total amount was not paid in full, substantial finance charges were accruing.

"Is this another mistake?" he thought to himself.

The pastor was thoroughly concerned when he opened another envelope that contained a monthly installment bill for two desktop computers. He looked around the offices and noticed a new desktop in the bookkeeper's office, but he couldn't find a second one. He looked through the office files again, but didn't see any paperwork that showed the church had purchased any computers.

The pastor laid the paperwork down and considered the possibilities: Could all of these bills be a mistake, or was something else going on? He decided he needed help to figure this out.

The auditor arrived the next week and began reviewing the church's financial files, including the suspicious bills that the pastor had received. After interviewing current staff and reviewing financial reports, general ledger details, bank statements, canceled checks, and other office files, the auditor had a clear understanding of the church's financial condition.

The pastor called a special board meeting and asked the auditor to join them. The auditor shared his findings with the board and revealed some disturbing news: The former pastor had used church funds for personal expenses and concealed this activity from the board and bookkeeper. The auditor proceeded to describe the depth and breadth of the abuse. The former pastor used church funds to make monthly payments on his personal charge accounts and credit cards. These payments were made through electronic fund transfers. Additionally, he had been using the church's charge accounts for his personal benefit.

To add insult to injury, the auditor explained that the abuse had significantly affected the church's cash flow. The abuse had become so rampant and encompassed so many accounts that there weren't enough funds each month to pay for these fraudulent transactions, let alone the church's valid expenses. As a result, the former pastor had to resort to making minimum payments on many of these accounts because the church's weekly cash flow wasn't enough to pay the entire amounts. This exacerbated the problem since the church was accruing finance charges and late fees that added to the outstanding balances.

The board members were visibly stunned and wondered how this was concealed from them. The auditor explained that the pastor's access to the bank accounts allowed him to make several electronic fund transfers each month. He picked up the mail each day, which included the monthly bills, credit card statements, and bank statements. The pastor would tell the bookkeeper which checks to write and for how much. Neither the bookkeeper nor board members saw the actual bills or statements. Unfortunately, while the board received a summary financial report each month, the report lacked sufficient details that would have allowed them to see this abuse.

The auditor explained that the pastor further concealed his activity by removing these monthly bills and statements from the church office. Support for many of the payments reflected on the church's bank statements could not be located in the church office. As a result, the auditor explained that the total amount of the abuse could not be calculated and suspected it was much larger. However, based on his review of the available documents, he determined the pastor's abuse consisted of:

- Using church funds to make electronic payments on three personal credit cards. (The monthly payments ranged from $100 to $500 for at least two years.)
- Spending up to $17,300 for personal items at a local wholesale club.
- Charging gasoline purchases to the church for family and friends—at least twenty-six purchases over a two-month period, and sometimes charging gas at multiple locations on the same day.
- Using church funds to pay for a computer that he gave to his wife.
- Incurring finance charges and late fees on the church's accounts totaling $4,000.

The board discussed how the church would recover and move forward. They decided against taking legal action but did provide the auditor's findings to the former pastor's ecclesiastical leadership. Unfortunately for the church, they had to make significant cutbacks in their planned spending over the next twelve months in order to pay off these outstanding balances.

WHAT WENT WRONG

In this case study, there was a lack of accountability and transparency in the church's financial operations. The former pastor was able to conceal his abuse of funds by having direct access to the bank account and bank statements. He also directed the bookkeeper to write checks and directed board members to sign checks without providing supporting documentation.

In the nonprofit world, trust is a much-desired character trait. I've often heard leaders say, "I give people my trust, until I have a reason not to." Certainly, this is a worthy attitude to have in our interpersonal relationships, but trust is not an effective control within the financial arena.

This church did not have sufficient controls to ensure that disbursements were proper and adequately supported. The former pastor had online access to the bank accounts and would pay several bills electronically without anyone knowing. The supporting invoices and monthly statements were not kept in the church office or provided to the board for review.

The former pastor would open the mail, pull out the bills, determine which ones should be paid, and give a list to the bookkeeper that contained the name of the vendor and the check amount. The bookkeeper would prepare the check, and a board member would sign the check and return it to the pastor for mailing. However, the person signing the check did not have the corresponding invoice to review when signing the check.

While the board received financial reports each month, they only received summary reports. They didn't have access to general ledger details that clearly identified all transactions. Without access to the invoices or general ledger details, many of the payments authorized by the former pastor (whether by check or electronic funds transfer) did not have an appropriate level of accountability and transparency.

BEST PRACTICES

Accountability and transparency are the key components of good stewardship. Because churches and nonprofits rely on donated funds to continue operations, these safeguards are crucial for donor confidence and will also protect church leaders from accusations of impropriety or self-dealing.

More importantly, accountability and transparency can help prevent unauthorized wire transfers, which is a common way for embezzlement to occur. Consider the following cases:

- A Virginia woman pleaded guilty to embezzling nearly $570,000 from the American Diabetes Association. For over nine years, the treasury manager initiated 133 unauthorized wire transfers from the association's bank account to a personal bank account that she controlled. To conceal her crime, she altered approved purchase request forms and accounting records to make the transfer look like legitimate expenses such as postage charges.[1]
- A grand jury indicted a forty-year-old woman for allegedly embezzling more than $453,000 from her employer. For almost three years, the employee initiated electronic fund transfers from the company's bank account into her own bank account.[2]

To make sure that all payments, including electronic fund transfers, are accountable and transparent at your church, consider the following controls:

- When paying by check, the bookkeeper should prepare checks for payment and a board member or other authorized signer should sign checks only after reviewing supporting invoices.

- When paying by electronic fund transfer, the invoice should be reviewed and approved by a board member or other authorized signer before payment. The board member should initial the invoice and make a note that it would be paid via an electronic payment.

- Supporting documentation should be filed by vendor, with either the check stub attached to the invoice or other notation that includes date paid and check number.

As an additional level of accountability, empower the bookkeeper and board members to ask for supporting documentation or additional details when preparing checks, signing checks, or recording the financial information. Further, a complete set of financial reports, including details of every transaction, should be provided to the governing board or the finance subcommittee each month.

EVALUATE YOUR ORGANIZATION

- Do you require the treasurer or board members to review supporting documentation before signing checks? Do they know what documentation is appropriate? What happens if adequate documentation isn't available?

- Do you require proper approval before making payments by electronic fund transfer? Who has authority to approve transfers? How is approval documented?

- Do you keep check stubs and supporting documentation for accountability and transparency? How long is documentation maintained? Where is it stored?

- Do you empower check signers to request additional support, if needed, when approving disbursements?

- Do you provide a complete set of financial reports, including general ledger details, to the governing board each month?

FOR FURTHER REVIEW

Would you like to know if your controls are strong enough to prevent embezzlement through electronic fund transfer from happening at your ministry? Review the internal audit program in Appendix B, and perform a mini-audit by completing the audit steps in the Bank Activity and Reconciliations section. Consider changes to policy or process to strengthen oversight of electronic expense payments if any weaknesses exist.

CREDIT CARD ABUSE

THE CHIEF FINANCIAL OFFICER (CFO) handed the business credit card to the new employee with a strict warning: "This is not a license to spend money indiscriminately. We have strict controls over the use of credit cards in our organization. This credit card is provided as a convenient way to make purchases; but those purchases must be approved in your departmental budget, and you must turn in receipts for each and every transaction. We have additional requirements regarding use, approval, and documentation in our policy manual. I expect you to read it and comply."

Fortunately, the CFO required all employees to follow the established policies. When the monthly credit card statement was received, all employees were expected to attach receipts, identify the business purpose of the expense, and note the appropriate account to charge the expense to. The accounts payable (AP) clerk was empowered to follow up with any employee who didn't follow the established procedures. That is, every employee except the CFO.

Over the years the AP clerk noticed that while all employees attached their receipts to the credit card statement, the CFO would place his receipts in an envelope and seal it before giving it to the clerk. The clerk was instructed to post all employees' expenses to the appropriate ledger and pay the monthly bill. However, the CFO stated that he would post the expenses for his own activity.

It seemed appropriate to her that the CFO would want to take an interest in the financials and post some of the activity. But now, as she scanned some of his activity, she became concerned. Many of the expenses didn't seem appropriate for their organization, and other employees didn't make similar purchases. She dismissed her concern by thinking, "Surely, the CFO would know what expenses were appropriate or not." However, the charges continued for several months, and the CFO continued to submit his receipts in a sealed envelope. The AP clerk continued to file the envelope away and make the payments. While her suspicion was growing month after month, she continued to dismiss it.

As the AP clerk reviewed the current month's credit card bill, her heart sank. The CFO had made a purchase that was clearly not business-related. Furthermore, the transaction was not appropriate for an employee of this nonprofit organization, let alone the CFO, who was also a minister. She knew it was time to let someone else know about her concerns.

As the AP clerk explained her concerns to the president of the organization, she showed him the CFO's credit card statement. The president confirmed that many of the transactions were not appropriate. He was surprised that the CFO sealed his receipts in an envelope while all others were expected to attach them to the statement; however, he admitted that he didn't require the CFO to submit his purchases for approval. Together, they reviewed the statements for the past twelve months. The president verified that multiple transactions each month were not appropriate and decided it was time to confront the CFO.

Faced with the evidence presented, the CFO admitted that he used the organization's credit card for personal purchases and offered to make restitution. The president agreed and stated that he would request an audit to determine the total amount.

An audit revealed that during a four-year period, the CFO charged at least $20,000 in personal expenses to the organization. However, it was apparent that the abuse had been occurring longer. The abuse included purchases at local home improvement stores, frequent lunches near the office, frequent coffee and snacks around town, large purchases at clothing stores, extravagant meals while on travel, Starbucks gift certificates, golf items, and movie rentals at hotels.

The president terminated the CFO's employment and implemented new controls to keep credit card abuse from happening again.

WHAT WENT WRONG

In this case study, the CFO had established very strong controls at this ministry. The accounts receivable and accounts payable functions were performed by separate people. Disbursements were properly approved and adequately supported with invoices before a check was written and signed. The bank reconciliations were performed by someone who didn't sign checks. All employees were required to provide receipts for all credit card transactions, which the chief financial officer reviewed for appropriateness.

Unfortunately, no one reviewed the CFO's credit card transactions. No one held him accountable for his purchases. When he deviated from the established policies that everyone else had to follow, no one stopped him. While he was empowered to question purchases made by other staff members, no one was empowered to question his purchases.

This lack of accountability allowed his abuse to continue for more than four years. Although the accounts payable clerk noticed his deviation from established procedures, suspicious transactions gave her the courage to blow the whistle.

BEST PRACTICES

Credit cards are certainly a convenient way to make business purchases. They don't require any approval before use and are accepted all over the world. Unfortunately, these benefits contribute to their frequent abuse.

However, just like other expenditures, credit cards require adequate substantiation for all business expenses. Oftentimes, though, it is hard to keep track of all those receipts—a fact that is especially handy if you are trying to conceal your activity.

Credit card statements must be supported with receipts. The credit card statement will reveal that a purchase was made, but in most cases, the item or service being purchased will not be very apparent. For example, the statement will reveal a purchase was made at a department store, but it will not describe the items purchased.

Further, in order to comply with IRS requirements for an accountable plan, actual receipts are required for credit card purchases. The business purpose will need to be identified. In addition, for any meals or entertainment expenses, the names of those attending need to be identified.

Besides providing adequate support for every credit card transaction, it is necessary to have each transaction reviewed to determine if the purchase is an appropriate business expense. Without the itemized receipt, the appropriateness of the transaction cannot be determined. In this case study, while the CFO reviewed the appropriateness of purchases for other staff members, no one was reviewing his purchases for appropriateness.

This case study revealed one leader's activity that was not transparent or accountable. To minimize this risk in your organization, foster a workplace environment where transparency is encouraged and accountability is welcomed. Create accountability measures between leadership members and empower staff to hold each other accountable.

EVALUATE YOUR ORGANIZATION

- Do you require receipts for all credit card transactions? What happens if receipts are not available?

- Do you note the business purpose of each transaction? Are staff members aware of what constitutes an acceptable business purpose for your organization?

- Do you identify the names of those attending meal and entertainment functions as the IRS requires?

- Do you require secondary review and approval of all transactions? Who performs this approval? What happens if a transaction doesn't comply with policy?

- Do you foster a workplace environment that encourages transparency and accountability? Do all leaders promote an ethical climate throughout the organization?

FOR FURTHER REVIEW

Would you like to know if your controls are strong enough to prevent credit card abuse from happening at your ministry? Review the internal audit program in Appendix B, and perform a mini-audit by completing the audit steps in the Credit Card and Charge Accounts section. Consider changes to policy or process to strengthen controls for credit card usage if any weaknesses exist.

CREDIT CARD REFUNDS

THE ACCOUNTS RECEIVABLE MANAGER walked into her office one morning and noticed the phone message lying on her desk. With a staff member home sick, she had come into the office early that morning to catch up on some work. She had a lot of work ahead of her if she was going to meet some pending deadlines.

The manager worked for a ministry organization that operated a bookstore where parishioners could purchase books, music, and Bible study materials. The manager and her staff were responsible for billing customers and processing credit card payments.

After reading the message, she decided to put aside the tasks she had planned to work on and spend some time researching this new matter. The phone message was from a customer who called to question why they had received a bill when they hadn't ordered any product.

Normally, the manager's accounting clerk would handle this issue, but he was at home recovering from the flu, so she decided to look into this customer's complaint.

The manager pulled a copy of the invoice and noticed that the customer hadn't purchased any product in quite a while. However, a credit card adjustment had been posted to the customer's account that was normally used to reverse a previous payment. This resulted in a "balance due," so the organization had sent a bill to the customer at the end of the month.

As the manager reviewed the supporting documentation, she realized the adjustment was probably incorrect because the documentation was referencing a transaction for a different customer. That seemed like a silly, yet honest mistake, so she decided to review the actual credit card refund to see if any more information was available. She discovered that the refund was posted to a different credit card — not the one associated with the customer who received the bill. But what puzzled her more was that her initials were used to approve the adjustment. However, she didn't remember making or approving the transaction. She thought to herself, "I've certainly messed up a customer account in the past, but how could we make two errors on one customer account?"

As she looked further at the credit card adjustment, she realized other refunds had been posted to this particular credit card. She did a quick search for this credit card number and couldn't find that it had ever been used to purchase product from the bookstore.

Now she was intrigued. "Why are we making refunds to a credit card that we've never seen?" she wondered.

One by one, the manager started looking at the different refunds that had been posted to the anonymous credit card. For every refund, she found a corresponding adjustment that was posted to a customer's account. The adjustments were made to look like the customer's previous credit card payment was being refunded. However, this also resulted in a balance due for the customer.

The manager grew suspicious. All the adjustments had her initials attached to the approval documents, but she was positive she hadn't approved any of these adjustments. Then the manager noticed something else tied to these refunds. A few days after the adjustments and credit card refunds were processed, another adjustment was posted to the customer's account that cleared the outstanding balance. This adjustment would "write off" the remaining balance.

A bad-debt write-off was used when a customer with an outstanding balance could not be located, or refused to pay their bill.

These were rarely used and could only be authorized by the manager. Looking at these customer accounts, she knew that she didn't approve any of these write-off adjustments. Now the manager was convinced something fraudulent was occurring; she also realized who the perpetrator was.

When the accounting clerk recovered from his illness and returned to work a few days later, the manager confronted him. With the mountain of evidence in front of him, he quickly admitted to the fraudulent scheme. He admitted that he would create fraudulent credit card adjustments and then post the refunds to his personal credit cards. Then, he would post a bad-debt write-off a few days later to clear the customer's outstanding balance and conceal his activity. He also admitted to forging the manager's initials for approving the adjustments and write-offs.

In a four-month period, he initiated seven fraudulent transactions that resulted in almost $5,000 being posted to four personal credit cards. The accounting clerk was terminated and agreed to make restitution in lieu of prosecution.

WHAT WENT WRONG

In this case study, several control weaknesses allowed the perpetrator to create fraudulent transactions and embezzle ministry funds, but the primary cause was poor segregation of duties. The accounting clerk had the ability to do several tasks that were incompatible when viewed through the lens of accountability.

The clerk was able to post adjustments to customer accounts, process refunds to credit cards, and write off bad debt. While some of the tasks were supposed to be reviewed and approved by the accounts receivable manager, the process was not controlled to make sure the manager saw every adjustment.

The manager would review printouts of the adjustments each day, but the clerk concealed his activity by destroying the printouts of his fake adjustments. The manager could have easily searched the electronic financial records for all adjustments to make sure she was reviewing and approving every adjustment, but she failed to do so.

She also failed to review and approve the credit card refunds. If she would have reviewed the credit card refunds, she would have noticed that the refunds were being posted to a different credit card than the one associated with the customer's account.

BEST PRACTICES

Billing schemes, which include this type of refund fraud, are common plots involving fraudulent disbursements of cash. A recent study found billing schemes make up 22 percent of all frauds, across all industries, involving asset misappropriation.[1] Billing schemes often last about twenty-four months before they are discovered and result in a median loss of about $100,000.[2]

Unfortunately, religious and charitable organizations experience this type of fraud more frequently. This same study found billing schemes made up 32.5 percent of frauds at religious and charitable organizations.[3]

Thankfully for this ministry, this credit card refund scheme only lasted four months before it was discovered. The accounting clerk's recent illness kept him from posting the last write-off adjustment that would clear the customer's outstanding balance. As a result, when the monthly invoices were processed, this customer still had a balance, so an invoice was printed and included in the monthly mailing. The phone message from this customer was the only clue that something was amiss.

Poor segregation of duties is the breeding ground for fraudulent activity. Unfortunately, many churches and nonprofits do not separate financial responsibilities and have poor segregation of duties. As a result of incompatible duties, employees are more easily able to pull off embezzlement schemes like this credit card refund fraud.

The ministry in this case study did have multiple accounting staff and was able to separate financial responsibilities. However, while the functions were split between the accounts receivable manager and the accounting clerk, a few more basic steps were needed to ensure all transactions were fully accountable and transparent.

If your church has businesses such as a bookstore or coffee shop or takes registrations for summer camps, retreats, or conferences, you have probably implemented some type of billing system for your church members and customers. With many consumers preferring the ease of credit cards for payment, accommodating them makes credit card fraud a likely risk as well. This case study highlights the importance of having strong controls over the collection, billing, and adjustment of your customer accounts.

The most important control is separating the responsibilities for billing and collections. This will make it more difficult for one person to fraudulently process customer payments and conceal the activity by altering customer invoices or posting adjustments to customer accounts.

Consider implementing the following controls to reduce the risk of this fraud occurring at your ministry:

- Require at least two people to be involved in the billing and collections process.
- Require all adjustments and refunds to be supported with proper documentation.
- Require management approval for any adjustments to a customer's balance, including the write-off of bad debt.
- Require management approval before processing refunds.
- Ensure credit card refunds are posted to the original credit card used to make the purchase. If the card number is not available, send a check to the customer's address on file for the amount of the refund.

EVALUATE YOUR ORGANIZATION

- Have you adequately separated the billing and collections process? Who performs these functions?

- Do you have separate individuals receiving payments, posting adjustments to customer accounts, and issuing credit card refunds? Who performs these functions?

- Do you require all adjustments and refunds to be supported with proper documentation? What constitutes proper documentation? What happens if documentation isn't available?

- Do you require management approval for any adjustments to a customer's balance? Who has authority to approve adjustments? How is approval documented?

- Do you require management approval when reducing a customer's accounts receivable balance? Who has authority to approve changes? How is approval documented?

- Do you require management approval before processing credit card refunds? Who has authority to approve refunds? How is approval documented?

- Do you post refunds to the same credit card used in the original transaction? If not, how do customers receive the refunds?

FOR FURTHER REVIEW

Would you like to know if your controls are strong enough to prevent billing fraud from happening at your ministry? Review the internal audit program in Appendix B, and perform a mini-audit by completing the audit steps in the Sales and Accounts Receivable section. Consider changes to policy or process to strengthen controls over collections, billing, and account adjustments if any weaknesses exist.

UNPAID PAYROLL TAXES

A S THE DISTRICT OFFICER looked around the room at the twenty-three employees of the church and affiliated school, his heart sank. He wished there was another option, but he knew there was no other solution available. He opened the meeting with some pleasantries and then proceeded to share the difficult news. "Due to mismanagement of church funds by the previous leadership," he began, "we have no other option but to close the church school and lay off all church and school employees immediately."

After the meeting, the district officer reflected that it was just a few months earlier when the phone on his desk rang. On the other end was the senior pastor of one of the churches in his district whom he helped mentor. The pastor shared some discouraging news: The IRS had placed a lien on his church for unpaid payroll taxes. If the church didn't rectify the situation now, the IRS was threatening to close the church and the affiliated school for kindergarten through grade 12. Unfortunately, the church didn't have the funds to pay the $400,000 tax bill and needed some help from the district office.

The pastor stated that he had no idea how this situation happened and explained that the church didn't have enough funds to pay their current bills, let alone the massive tax bill, and he didn't know where else to turn. To complicate matters, he stated that the bookkeeper had unexpectedly resigned.

The district officer agreed to visit the church to assess their situation. Knowing that the bookkeeper had just resigned, he brought an investigative team with him, including an accountant with experience in banking, auditing, and taxes. It didn't take long for the accountant to figure out that the church had been properly withholding payroll taxes from their employees' wages but failing to remit the taxes to the IRS. In fact, the church had been withholding taxes for the past six years without remitting them to the IRS. The church was submitting W–2 forms each year, but not the corresponding Form 941 (Employer's Quarterly Federal Tax Return), so it didn't take the IRS very long to figure out the problem. The church soon began to receive notices of delinquency from the IRS that had continued for six years until the IRS finally took additional action and placed a lien on the church.

It was soon apparent to the district officer that the pastor was not only aware of the tax situation but also complicit in the tax evasion. A review of the church financial records revealed that the pastor was spending more money than the church was receiving in contributions. He didn't allow the bookkeeper to remit the taxes to the IRS because he was spending the funds on other things. Furthermore, the board was aware of the delinquent taxes because they often discussed it during board meetings.

Before the bookkeeper resigned, she tried to conceal her involvement in this scheme by destroying payroll documents and erasing a computer hard drive that contained the church's financial records. Fortunately, the investigative team was able to recover the financial records from the online backup provider and recreate the payroll documents.

The investigative team also discovered abuse in other financial areas. To hide the fact that he was hiring employees who were not eligible to work in the United States, the pastor had proxy (or ghost) employees on the payroll account. Each week, the church would pay these proxy employees, who would then cash the check and provide the funds to the person who actually worked at the church. The pastor also had a significant amount of expenses paid with a church credit card that were not supported with receipts or properly justified as business expenses. When the church's income could no longer cover his extravagant and excessive spending, he started transferring funds from the school to cover the church expenses. Unfortunately for him, the funds had run out, and the IRS got tired of waiting.

As a result of this abuse, the church was forced to take extreme measures to address the lien. They had to lay off twenty-three church and school employees, close the school, and send one hundred students to other schools. It took another four months to pay off all the vendors. Additionally, the pastor and his wife were fired and lost their home.

Two years later, the church was still struggling to pay the tax bill but had managed to move forward with a part-time secretary and a pro bono pastor. The former pastor and bookkeeper were still being investigated by the IRS for their involvement in this fraud.

WHAT WENT WRONG

In this case study, leaders entrusted to oversee the church finances failed to manage those finances responsibly and comply with applicable laws and regulations. Several failures by leadership allowed this abuse to occur, which included:

- Failing to operate ethically in all aspects of church administration, including the hiring of employees.
- Failing to ensure applicable taxes were promptly remitted to the IRS.
- Failing to ensure required IRS Forms 941 were submitted to the IRS.
- Failing to create and execute a balanced budget for the church.
- Failing to hold the pastor and staff accountable for how funds were spent, including purchases made on church credit cards.

Most fraud cases are committed by sole perpetrators. One six-year study of fraud schemes found 85 percent were committed by one person.[1] Having several people involved, known as collusion, is rare. However, in this case, several people knew this deceit was occurring and colluded to keep it going, including the pastor, the bookkeeper, and the board members. Unfortunately, no one was willing to take their fiduciary responsibilities seriously and put a stop to this scheme. In the end, many innocent people suffered the consequences of their leaders' misconduct.

BEST PRACTICES

Payroll tax reporting can be confusing. Regardless of whether an organization is for-profit or not-for-profit, the IRS has several reporting requirements for organizations with employees. For example, employers must withhold federal income taxes and Social Security taxes from their employees' wages and deposit those taxes with the IRS. For smaller organizations, taxes are submitted monthly, but for larger organizations, the payroll taxes must be remitted to the IRS on a weekly basis. Additionally, employers must file quarterly tax returns (Form 941) and issue annual Wage and Tax Statements (Form W–2) to employees.

Employees must complete the Employee's Withholding Allowance Certificate (Form W–4) to claim withholding allowances, which determines the amount of income tax that should be withheld from their wages.

Further, when hiring employees, the government requires employers to verify that the employee is eligible to work in the United States. For any employee hired after November 6, 1986, an Employment Eligibility Verification (Form I–9) should be completed.

Most churches are subject to the withholding requirements, though some exceptions exist for ministerial staff, contributing to the confusion. For example, ministers are treated as employees for federal tax reporting, but are exempt from federal tax withholding. However, if they would like to have federal taxes voluntarily withheld by the church, they should fill out a W–4 form.

Because payroll can be so confusing, some churches outsource their payroll process to a local accounting firm or third-party payroll provider. However, the church is still responsible to make sure payroll taxes are properly remitted to the IRS. One fraudulent payroll service in New York collected over $3 million in payroll taxes from 1,100 small businesses and nonprofits but failed to remit the taxes to the IRS. Instead, the president used the funds for operating expenses and personal expenditures.[2,3] While he was sentenced to eight years in prison and ordered to make restitution, his clients are still liable for the unpaid taxes.[4]

To make sure your payroll taxes are properly deposited with the IRS, employers can sign up for the Treasury Department's Electronic Federal Tax Payment Service at https://www.eftps.gov/eftps/. This free service allows users to go online to pay taxes or see what tax deposits have been made. Whether you handle your own payroll or outsource it, visiting this website should be a part of your monthly internal control process.

While it may seem that the IRS has too many regulations, they do offer a wealth of information to help nonprofits navigate the vast sea of requirements. They have a website dedicated to churches and other religious organizations, covering a wide range of topics that includes a quick-reference tax guide, details about annual filing requirements, and a discussion on prohibited activities and unrelated business income tax. If you want to know more about these topics, visit their website at http://www.irs.gov/Charities-&-Non-Profits/ Churches-&-Religious-Organizations.

EVALUATE YOUR ORGANIZATION

- Do you have properly completed and signed Forms I–9 and W–4 for each employee?

- Do you remit payroll taxes promptly? Who performs this function?

- Do you submit IRS Form 941 quarterly? Who performs this function?

- Do you operate within a balanced budget? How often is financial activity reviewed? Who is responsible to manage and oversee financial activity?

- Does someone separate from the payroll process ensure payroll taxes are deposited and required forms are submitted? Who performs this review? How often?

FOR FURTHER REVIEW

Would you like to know if your controls are strong enough to prevent tax-related misappropriations from happening at your ministry? Review the internal audit program in Appendix B, and perform a mini-audit by completing the audit steps in the Payroll section. Consider changes to policy or process to strengthen the accountability for the payment of IRS payroll taxes if any weaknesses exist.

PETTY CASH AND
TUITION PAYMENTS

A S THE MINISTRY LEADER walked out of the office, the business administrator was perplexed. This was the third church employee to report that cash or other items had gone missing from their office. The business administrator turned around in his chair and reflected on what he had been told the last few weeks.

One employee had stated that a small MP3 player was missing from a desk. At first, the business administrator thought a small item like an MP3 player could easily be misplaced and might show up at a later date. But another employee stated that their petty cash was missing. The administrator was certainly concerned about the missing funds but thought it was probably an isolated incident. After what the ministry leader had told him today, he was truly concerned there might be a bigger problem at hand.

This ministry leader led the preschool department. She had related to the business administrator that a few parents had called to ask if the preschool had received their tuition payment the previous month. The parents had noticed that even though a few weeks had passed, their tuition checks had not cleared the bank. Unfortunately, the preschool office didn't have a record of receiving a recent payment from these parents. Additionally, the accounts payable clerk had been contacting parents who were delinquent in paying their tuition. Some of these parents were reporting that they had indeed paid their tuition payments in the past few weeks.

The business administrator decided he needed to do more investigation. After the administrator talked with the preschool employees, they contacted some of these parents again and asked a few probing questions. Some parents had paid their tuition with cash, while others had paid with a check. However, all the parents had one thing in common: they stated that they had placed their tuition payments in the drop box next to the preschool office.

As a convenience for parents, the preschool had installed a drop box next to the preschool office so parents could still make their tuition payments if no one was available in the office. The drop box was a metal box with a locking lid. In the top of the lid, there was a small cutout to insert payment envelopes.

As the business administrator looked at the drop box, he tested the lock and found that it was strong and secure. But he noticed that while the opening in the lid was not big enough for his hand to slip in, a smaller hand might be able to reach in. He thought to himself, "I wonder if someone is reaching into the box and removing the tuition payments?"

The church had security cameras, so he decided to visit with the IT director and see if the cameras had recorded any activity that could help shed light on this perplexing situation. When he visited with the IT director, he asked to see footage of activity near the preschool drop box. The IT director looked confused and stated, "I didn't know we had a preschool drop box." When the preschool had installed the drop box, they didn't think to notify the IT director that a camera should be pointed at the new drop box, since it would be holding cash and checks overnight.

The IT director and business administrator discussed another plan. They would secretly install a camera in the area and see if they could capture anyone who might be stealing the tuition payments.

That day, they placed a portable stereo with a hidden camera inside near the office area. The hidden camera had a clear view of the drop box and the nearby office area. As additional bait, they placed a small amount of cash in one of the desk drawers. They even documented the serial numbers of each bill in case they would need to identify the cash later.

The next day, the business administrator and IT director reviewed the video footage. The camera did indeed capture someone stealing the tuition payments, but the church leaders were surprised at who the culprit was.

The video showed a man entering the preschool office area and heading directly for the tuition drop box. The man was able to stick part of his hand into the slot in the lid, but he wasn't able to reach any of the envelopes. The man then looked around the office and found two long, flat objects to assist him. He used these two objects that looked like a letter opener or ruler as tongs to reach into the drop box and carefully remove the contents.

The man then continued to pilfer the office by opening several drawers, looking for other items to steal. The man found the stack of cash that was placed in the drawer as bait. He took the cash and, satisfied that he had everything he wanted, then left the area.

What surprised the church leaders most was that this man was part of the nighttime cleaning crew. For the past several months, a local vendor had been providing the cleaning service for the church. One of the reasons the church selected this vendor to perform the cleaning service was because the vendor performed background checks on their employees. Knowing that background checks were performed, the church leaders were certainly surprised that someone from this company would steal from the church.

The business administrator contacted the owner of the cleaning service and presented his evidence. After viewing the evidence, the company owner assured the business administrator that appropriate action would be taken. It didn't take very long for the owner to call for a company-wide meeting and, in front of all the employees, fire the man who had stolen funds from the church.

WHAT WENT WRONG

In this case study, the church had implemented some new processes for the convenience of their employees and the families who attended the preschool. However, leaders failed to embed safeguards within those new processes. While these new actions were meant to improve and streamline processes, they actually exposed the church to more risk.

The first security pitfall was that the church had allowed some ministry leaders to have petty cash funds. While appropriate procedures were put in place on how the funds should be used, there were not appropriate procedures in place to safeguard those funds. The business administrator found that there were several petty cash funds within the church, and many of the funds were not fully protected. Some were placed in office drawers or filing cabinets that didn't lock. As a result, these funds were at risk of being stolen by other employees, visitors, or vendors.

For the convenience of the families who attended their preschool, the church installed a drop box for tuition payments. However, the drop box wasn't very secure, and the opening in the lid was large enough that someone was able to remove the contents in the drop box with very little effort.

Further, although the church had security cameras throughout the building, no one notified the IT director that a new cash container was being installed in the church so that a camera could be placed in the area for better accountability.

After further consideration and review of the church's processes, the business administrator made a few changes. Many of the petty cash funds were consolidated into one fund so that the fund could be secured at all times, thereby reducing the risk of theft. A new preschool drop box was installed that had a much smaller opening in the top to eliminate the potential for hands or other objects to reach in and remove tuition payments. Additionally, a camera was installed near the preschool drop box.

As he reviewed these processes, the administrator also determined some departments were holding on to revenue for extended periods of time. This revenue was collected for T-shirt sales or event registrations and was being held by the ministry departments for up to thirty days. This increased the risk of theft or abuse since the departmental offices weren't as secure as the main office where the safe was located. As a result, the administrator instituted a new policy that required all revenue and tuition payments be placed in the office safe each night. Since the safe had a drop box feature, money could be placed in the safe even if no one was in the business office.

BEST PRACTICES

A petty cash fund is a small amount of money that is maintained within the church for unplanned or minor disbursements. A petty cash fund is like a safety net: in case of emergencies, cash is available to make a purchase, reimburse an employee, or pay an invoice. Petty cash is meant to be used when the normal purchase process or reimbursement process cannot be followed, such as when an unexpected need arises, but no one is available to approve or sign a check. In these instances, having some petty cash available will allow the purchase to be made without impeding the operation of the church. Unfortunately, for quick and easy access, the petty cash fund is often kept in an office drawer or in a filing cabinet with minimal security. And most employees know where the petty cash fund is stored. Consequently, even though many petty cash funds are low in value, they can be easily abused or stolen.

Installing offering collection boxes around the church is a

convenient way for attenders to make contributions after the service or make tuition payments when office personnel aren't available. However, safeguards are needed when placing collection boxes within the church since cash and checks are left in the unattended containers for long periods of time. While some churches install sturdy metal containers made specifically for this purpose and permanently affix the collection box to the floor or wall, others will create a drop box in an office door or repurpose an existing box as a collection point. Oftentimes, these homemade or repurposed collection boxes are not as sturdy or secure.

Stealing cash and checks from a collection box is a fraud scheme known as skimming. As noted in case study one, skimming is one of the more frequent ways funds are stolen from an organization. According to the ACFE fraud study, skimming occurred in 11.8 percent of fraud cases reviewed, caused a median loss of $40,000 per case, and the schemes lasted eighteen months before being discovered.[1] But at religious organizations who participated in the study, skimming occurred more often, or in 12.5 percent of the cases reviewed.[2]

Stealing petty cash funds is known as a cash-on-hand fraud scheme. This scheme is another common scheme to steal funds from an organization. Similar to skimming schemes, the ACFE study determined that cash-on-hand schemes occurred in 11.9 percent of fraud cases reviewed.[3] Although cash-on-hand schemes resulted in a lower median loss of $18,000, these schemes were perpetrated just as long as skimming schemes (eighteen months) before being discovered.[4] As with skimming, at religious organizations who participated in the study, cash-on-hand schemes occurred in 12.5 percent of the cases reviewed.[5]

These statistics reveal the reasons why churches need to have strong and effective controls over petty cash funds and cash collection boxes.

To minimize the impact of abuse or theft, a petty cash fund should be small in value: maybe $50, $100, or $200, depending on the church's needs. Petty cash funds should be assigned to one person who will act as the custodian of the fund. This person is responsible for maintaining the cash, granting access, recording activity, and reconciling the account. Further, petty cash funds should be stored in a secure area, with limited access from most employees and volunteers.

Unattended collection boxes should be made of sturdy materials and securely affixed to the floor or wall. The container should have a strong lock, and the opening should be just big enough to allow an envelope to pass through, but not so large that a hand or other object could pass through to remove items in the container.

EVALUATE YOUR ORGANIZATION

- Before hiring outside vendors, do you require the vendor to perform background checks on their employees who will be working inside the church, especially if they have access to offices at night or other areas with expensive equipment, like the sound booth, auditorium platform, or storage areas? Do you require the vendor to verify to the church that these background checks have been completed before one of their employees works on church premises?

- Can you reduce the number of petty cash funds used at the church? Should you consider consolidating several petty cash funds into one central fund? Are petty cash funds stored in a locked container and properly secured at night?

- Are your cash collection boxes securely fastened to the floor or wall? Are the openings large enough for envelopes to pass through but not large enough for a hand or other object to pass through and remove contents? How often are the collection boxes emptied? By whom? Are the contents moved to a more secure location, like the office safe, if not immediately counted and deposited?

- Do you have a secure safe in the office area, preferrably with a drop box feature, so that ministry departments can turn in cash on a nightly basis?

- Have you installed cameras throughout the building to monitor activity and increase accountability? Do all sensitive areas have cameras installed, including those areas where donations are collected and counted, where collection boxes are installed, and where the office safe is located? Who monitors the camera feeds? How many hours of activity are recorded and archived?

FOR FURTHER REVIEW

Would you like to know if your controls are strong enough to prevent skimming and cash-on-hand theft from happening at your ministry? Review the internal audit program in Appendix B, and perform a mini-audit by completing the audit steps in the Contributions and Cash Receipts section and the Petty Cash section. Consider changes to policy or process to strengthen safeguards for petty cash funds and cash box collections if any weaknesses exist.

MISSING ASSETS

A S HER HUSBAND walked into the house, she could see he was struggling to carry a large box. The box in his arms was almost too big for him to carry, but he managed to carry it through the door and set it down in the living room. Once she realized what it was, she squealed with delight. "Where did you get the television?" she asked. "It's so big—and just what we've wanted."

"You won't believe it!" he exclaimed. "The church bought this flat screen television for the nursery, but they decided they didn't need it. I asked the nursery director what they were going to do with it, and she said we could have it!"

Her husband worked at the church taking care of equipment and building maintenance. She was very thankful for her husband's job. This gift from the church was a blessing to their family. In fact, she felt that there had been a number of blessings lately. She thought about the extra money they had for Christmas gifts and the first family vacation in years. Even though she knew the church couldn't pay her husband a lot of money, she was very happy with how the two of them were able to find extra funds when needed.

The next Sunday, as she walked her child to his Sunday School class, she bumped into the nursery director. "I'm so glad I ran into you," she said. "I wanted to thank you for giving us that television. We are so excited and thankful." The nursery director politely smiled and responded, "You're welcome." But with a puzzled look on her face, quickly followed up with, "I'm sorry, but what television are you referring to?"

After repeating what her husband had told her, the woman quickly realized that the nursery director didn't have a clue about the television. She offered a quick apology, saying, "I'm sorry, I thought that's what my husband told me, but I must be mistaken." After a brief conversation, the mother quickly excused herself.

After church, she recalled the conversation with the nursery director. She was confused, but tried to dismiss her concern. Unfortunately, her concern lingered. She thought about the past few months. "Where did her husband get the extra cash to pay for the family vacation they had always dreamed of?" she wondered. "Was the family receiving some unexpected blessings, or was something else happening?"

After a few days, the lingering uncertainty and concern finally overwhelmed her. As her husband walked through the doorway after work, she confronted him. She repeated the conversation she had with the nursery director and then listed all the extra "blessings" they had received over the past few months.

Realizing that his story was unraveling, the husband decided it was time to come clean. Over the next hour, he proceeded to tell his wife how he had been stealing items from the church, selling them on eBay, and keeping the cash.

He began his confession by stating that this scheme had started out with honest motives. As he worked around the church, he realized there was a lot of equipment, props, and other items that weren't needed anymore. Although he didn't ask for approval, he thought it would be helpful if he sold some of these unused items on eBay. After the first sale, he put the cash in the offering. When the next item sold, he realized he could use the funds to purchase a piece of equipment for his department that was not included in the current budget. He felt justified to do this since he wasn't really using additional funds for the purchase—he was merely trading one piece of equipment for another.

However, he soon realized that this endeavor could become a lucrative side business. Clearly, no one was keeping track of the equipment put into storage, and no one had even noticed that he had sold two items or placed extra cash in the offering. He tested his theory and sold one more item, waiting to see if anyone noticed. After a few days had passed, he was convinced no one was paying attention to all the excess equipment in storage.

It didn't take him long to escalate his scheme and start selling multiple items on eBay. After a few months of selling pieces of equipment, props, and lighting, he had accumulated over $17,000 in extra cash.

The next day, a humbled and ashamed employee confessed his scheme to church leadership and offered to pay restitution. Thankfully for him, his boss offered him some mercy and allowed him to keep his job as long as restitution was made over the next few months. The church was forced to make some immediate changes to their inventory process, including creating a list of all inventory items, assigning a person to oversee all assets, and instituting regular inventory audits.

WHAT WENT WRONG

In this case study, the church failed to implement basic inventory and asset controls. While purchasing fixed assets and equipment made up a significant portion of the church's annual expenditures, the church had weak controls in place to protect those assets. Many of the church's assets had value, both for resale and for personal use, which made them a prospective target. Unfortunately, the church lacked a complete process to ensure all assets were properly safeguarded and accounted for.

Even though the church had a list of some fixed assets, employees at the church had access to storage areas and were able to remove unused assets without anyone noticing. The church didn't have a process to make sure the inventory list was up to date nor to perform random checks to ensure assets were still in the building.

BEST PRACTICES

Fixed asset purchases are usually a significant portion of a church's annual budget. The types of items that churches need for operation and ministry are almost limitless, including audio and video equipment, lighting and stage equipment, televisions, computers, monitors, tables, chairs, and office supplies. The significant resale value of these assets is one reason that fixed asset and equipment theft is a serious problem for any organization, including a church.

Further, these assets are difficult to protect. Many churches remain open during the week for appointments, rehearsals, or personal meditation and prayer, allowing church members and visitors to enter the building with little notice. Auditoriums remain open, and audio and video equipment is usually sitting on the stage or in the sound booth. Equipment storage rooms inside the church may be locked, but the same key that opens employee offices may open the storage room as well. Further, assets and equipment in garages and sheds are locked but are not guarded at night.

The difficulty in protecting assets and equipment is the main reason that non-cash frauds are a significant risk for most organizations, including churches. While the ACFE study found that such non-cash misappropriations occurred in 15 percent of the fraud cases reviewed at religious organizations, it occurred in 21 percent of all cases reviewed and had a median loss of $95,000.[1] Unfortunately, discovering the non-cash fraud schemes took an average of twelve months for these organizations.[2]

Strong controls are a key ingredient in ensuring that church assets do not go missing. Churches should make sure that someone has the responsibility to maintain a fixed asset inventory list. This person becomes the fixed asset custodian. The custodian should include on the asset inventory list all assets over a certain threshold (e.g., $500 or $1,000). As inventory or equipment above the threshold is purchased, the item should be added to the asset list. As items are disposed of, given away, or sold, they should be removed from the asset list. On an annual or other periodic basis, the fixed asset custodian should test a sampling of assets on the list to determine whether the items still exist. In lieu of visually inspecting every item on the list, the custodian can ask each ministry leader to verify that certain fixed assets are still in their possession. Of course, whether these fixed assets are stored in a garage, shed or throughout the building, the assets should be secured.

EVALUATE YOUR ORGANIZATION

- Does your church maintain a fixed asset inventory list? Who is responsible for keeping it current? How are assets put on the inventory list, and when are assets removed from the list?
- Does your church have a policy of what value of assets they will include on a fixed asset inventory? Is the value too high or too low?
- Does your church perform a random sample of items on the fixed asset inventory list to determine if the items are still in the church's possession? How often does this review occur? Who is in charge of performing the review? Does this person visually inspect each item or just ask another ministry leader for confirmation? Is the review adequate?
- Are fixed assets properly secured when not in use? Are storage rooms, sheds, and garages locked at all times? Who has keys to these storage areas, and why?

FOR FURTHER REVIEW

Would you like to know if your controls are strong enough to prevent non-cash theft from happening at your ministry? Review the internal audit program in Appendix B, and perform a mini-audit by completing the audit steps in the Property and Insurance section. Consider changes to policy or process to strengthen review of asset inventories if any weaknesses exist.

EXTRA PAYROLL CHECKS

THE EXECUTIVE PASTOR continued to stare at his computer screen, analyzing the financial report he had just created. The report detailed the payroll activity for the church staff for the past twelve months. Something didn't look right, and he needed to talk to the bookkeeper. He had a sinking feeling that he wasn't going to enjoy this conversation.

Just four months prior, church leadership had decided it was time to hire an executive pastor. They chose an individual who had been serving in the church for many years. Not only was this individual familiar with their church culture, but he had the education and professional experience to perform this role. As he settled into his new role, he relied on the knowledge and training he received while completing his MBA to review the financial systems in place at the church.

He quickly determined that too much control and authority was centralized in the bookkeeping office. The bookkeeper was a longtime member of the church and had performed the bookkeeping function for almost ten years. As he reviewed the financial process, he determined a few internal controls were in place but quickly realized the bookkeeper had total control over much of the finances, with little accountability over her work.

With regard to existing controls, the bookkeeper entered transactions in the financial software and printed checks when bills had to be paid. The bookkeeper could not sign checks, so a board member would sign all checks. Additionally, while the bookkeeper reconciled the bank accounts, a board member would review and approve the bank reconciliation report. These controls allowed a second set of eyes to see and approve each transaction. But the executive pastor believed additional controls could be added to improve accountability, not only to protect the church's assets, but also to protect the employees.

The executive pastor decided more of the bookkeeping function should be segregated and split among two or more people, so he started to make some suggestions. He suggested the secretary could maintain control over the blank check stock and the bookkeeper would have to request a specific number of checks for that week's disbursements. He suggested the reconciliation function could be performed by another staff member. And he suggested that the payroll function could be outsourced to reduce the workload of the bookkeeper and the related overtime.

What surprised the executive pastor was the bookkeeper's reaction to each of these suggestions. The bookkeeper disliked every suggestion made by the executive pastor and pushed back against the need to segregate her duties. At first, the executive pastor thought the bookkeeper felt threatened that her job might be eliminated or that her contribution at the church wasn't valued. He was surprised that she continued to fight the new changes, even after he made a guarantee that her job was not in jeopardy and reassured her that she was a valuable staff member. After three months of ongoing conflict, the executive pastor grew concerned that the bookkeeper's resistance was due to something more sinister than a fear of losing some responsibilities.

As the executive pastor reviewed current financial reports, he noticed that the wages and salaries account was over budget. However, he had been told that over the past year, as the church leaders scrutinized the budget, several edicts had gone forth that overtime should be used sparingly and only approved on a case by case basis. Surprised at the overage, the executive pastor logged into the financial software to do more research. He theorized overtime was the culprit and decided to run the payroll report for the past twelve months to see which department, or departments, were incurring overtime.

As he stared at the report, he realized his conclusion about overtime was wrong. While there was some overtime incurred, he quickly identified why the wages and salary account was over budget. The church staff was paid biweekly, meaning they received a paycheck 26 times a year. A quick scan of the payroll report revealed that one of the church employees had received almost 40 paychecks in the past year—and it was the bookkeeper.

Before confronting the bookkeeper, the executive pastor invited a team of independent auditors in to confirm his suspicions. After reviewing the church's financial reports and testing key controls, the audit team confirmed the bookkeeper had been issuing extra payroll checks to herself for at least seven years. The auditors also determined the bookkeeper manipulated the payroll system and placed misleading documents in the payroll file in an attempt to conceal her activity if anyone happened to review the payroll reports.

The auditors estimated that over seven years, the bookkeeper received about 95 extra payroll checks, totaling at least $75,000.

The bookkeeper resigned before the auditors completed their review, but church leadership did confront the bookkeeper. In front of her husband and church leaders, the bookkeeper admitted to the scheme, signed a confession, and offered restitution.

In lieu of prosecution, the church leaders offered the bookkeeper forgiveness and restoration.

WHAT WENT WRONG

In this case study, one person had total control of the organization's finances. Although some good controls were in place at the church, the controls were not working effectively. For example:

- The bookkeeper printed checks but did not sign them. A board member, usually the treasurer, signed the checks. However, this control was weakened significantly because the board member had a signature stamp that was used to sign the checks. The signature stamp was kept in the possession of the bookkeeper. When the bookkeeper printed the extra payroll checks, she didn't need the treasurer to come in and sign checks; she already had access to the treasurer's signature stamp.

- When the executive pastor queried the board members about the quality of their review when they signed checks, most agreed that they didn't review the checks or the supporting invoices in detail. They performed a cursory review but agreed it wasn't enough to hold the bookkeeper accountable.

- Additionally, the executive pastor determined that none of the board members could recall signing payroll checks. In all likelihood, the bookkeeper didn't even present the payroll checks to a board member for signature. She probably used the signature stamp for all payroll checks.

- Further, while a board member would review the bank reconciliation report, the board members admitted to the executive pastor that they didn't review the reports in detail, didn't review the outstanding deposits or checks, and didn't scrutinize the itemized check listing nor review the bank statement for suspicious activity.

- Lastly, the executive pastor determined that while the book-keeper wasn't supposed to sign checks, she had complete online access to the church's bank account. Through the online access, the bookkeeper was able to transfer funds in and out of the church account with little scrutiny or accountability.

BEST PRACTICES

Salaries and wages is one of the most significant expense categories at a church. Payroll fraud is very easy to commit and can take several forms, including reporting more hours than actually worked, claiming overtime hours when not authorized, changing wage rates without approval, or adding a bonus payment without authorization. Payroll fraud is easily concealed when one person has total control over the payroll function and no one is reviewing the payroll activity for accountability.

The ACFE study found that organizations in the study affected by payroll fraud had a median loss of $50,000, occurring in 10.2 percent of the cases reviewed, and lasting twenty-four months before being detected.[1] Unfortunately, religious organizations might be more susceptible to payroll fraud. At religious organizations included in the study, payroll fraud occurred in 20 percent of the cases reviewed.[2]

For this reason, churches need to have strong controls over the payroll process and ensure salaries and wages are accurately calculated and reported. For example, employee wages should be approved by leadership and documented in the employee's personnel file. Time cards should be completed by hourly employees, signed by the employee, and approved by their supervisor. Whether employees receive an actual check or receive payment through direct deposit, someone in leadership should review the payroll journal to ensure each employee's paycheck is appropriate.

EVALUATE YOUR ORGANIZATION

- Does your church have a process to ensure salaries and wages are accurately calculated and reported? What is this process? Who is involved?

- Are employee wages approved by leadership? Who gives approval?

- Are employee wages documented and maintained in the employee's personnel file?

- Do hourly employees complete time cards for each pay period? Are employees required to sign the time card? Does a supervisor approve the time card?

- Do employees receive an actual check or direct deposit? If an employee receives an actual check, who creates the check? Who signs the check? Who delivers the check? If an employee receives pay by direct deposit, does someone review the ACH deposit to ensure it is complete and accurate?

- Is the payroll journal or detail report reviewed by someone in leadership to ensure that the total payroll is complete and appropriate? Who performs this review? How often is it performed?

FOR FURTHER REVIEW

Would you like to know if your controls are strong enough to prevent payroll fraud from happening at your ministry? Review the internal audit program in Appendix B, and perform a mini-audit by completing the audit steps in the Payroll section. Consider changes to policy or process to strengthen oversight and review of payroll records if any weaknesses exist.

PERFORMING A FRAUD
RISK ASSESSMENT

AFTER READING CHAPTER 4, you may be wondering if your financial practices are exposing your organization to the risk of fraud. One way to evaluate your fraud risk is to complete the following Fraud Risk Assessment. Answer the questions honestly and then score yourself using the instructions provided at the end of the assessment. Your score will help you identify risk areas—those areas that have weak internal controls, or where controls are missing or not working as expected.

After you complete the assessment, I encourage you to have a few of your leaders complete the assessment too. Include several people who are involved in the bookkeeping function or who are responsible for reviewing and approving the bookkeeping function. This group would include current accounting and bookkeeping staff, finance committee members, and board members.

Oftentimes, I find pastors and nonprofit leaders think their control processes are stronger than they actually are. By asking your frontline experts to complete the questionnaire, you may get a different view of controls and whether they are working as expected.

Once the assessment is completed and reviewed, you and your team can work on integrating those controls that your organization is lacking, increasing accountability and transparency in your financial operations.

FRAUD RISK ASSESSMENT FOR CHURCHES AND NONPROFITS

General Asset Controls	Yes	No	Sometimes	Comments
1. Financial policies and procedures are documented and current.				
2. Employees with access to cash or financial transactions are properly trained and supervised.				
3. Volunteers with access to cash or financial transactions are properly trained and supervised.				
4. The church maintains an up-to-date inventory record of noncash assets, fixed assets, buildings, and equipment.				
5. Periodic reviews are performed to test the accuracy of the fixed asset inventory records.				

	Yes	No	Sometimes	Comments
6. Regular reviews are performed to determine if insurance coverage is adequate and up-to-date.				
7. Insurance coverage includes theft by employees or volunteers; if not, employees and volunteers who handle cash are bonded.				

Contributions and Cash Receipts	Yes	No	Sometimes	Comments
1. Attendees have access to offering envelopes or online giving options to increase accountability in the collection process.				
2. While cash is maintained at the church, it is protected in a safe or an immoveable lock box.				
3. Contributions and other cash receipts are counted in a secure area.				

4. A team of at least two people collect and count all contributions and cash receipts.					
5. Money counters verify the contents of the offering envelopes with the amount written on the envelope.					
6. Checks are endorsed "for deposit only" along with the church's bank account.					
7. Contributions and other income are deposited within 24 hours.					
8. Cash is never taken out of the offering to pay for expenses.					
9. A summary count sheet, detailing the amount of cash, checks, and coins, is prepared by the counting team.					

10. The summary count sheet is signed by the members of the counting team.				
11. The counting team prepares the deposit slip.				
12. The deposit (cash, checks, and coin) is secured in a locking bank bag or tamper-proof bag while being transported to the bank.				
13. The person transporting the deposit to the bank does not have the ability to open the bank bag or tamper with the deposit without being detected.				
14. Someone not involved in the counting or deposit process reconciles the summary count sheet, deposit slip, and bank deposit receipt.				

15. Donations for restricted purposes are properly identified and recorded in the accounting records.					
16. Contributions are recorded to the donor records on a timely basis.					
17. Donor contribution records are reconciled to total contributions recorded in the general ledger.					
18. Contribution records are sent to donors on a regular or annual basis.					
19. The contribution receipt itemizes any contribution of $250 or more.					
20. The contribution receipt includes a statement that no goods or services were provided in exchange for the contribution, other than intangible religious benefits, if that is the case.					

Payments and Cash Disbursements	Yes	No	Sometimes	Comments
1. A purchase or check request is required before a purchase is made.				
2. The purchase or check request is properly approved by someone in leadership.				
3. When purchase requests are not used, someone other than the check preparer reviews and approves payment.				
4. Invoices are reviewed and approved by an authorized person who validates item was received (or service was provided) and amount is correct for payment.				
5. Payments are made from original invoices, not copies or estimates.				

6. Checks are signed when accompanied by proof that invoice is correct and appropriate to pay.				
7. If a signature stamp is used to sign checks, the person who prepares the check does not have access to the signature stamp. (If a signature stamp is not used, mark this question as "Yes.")				
8. All disbursements are made from prenumbered checks.				
9. Supporting documents and invoices are marked "paid" when checks are issued or archived in a manner that they cannot be presented for payment again.				
10. Voided checks are marked "voided," retained, and accounted for.				

11. Blank check stock is safeguarded at all times.				
12. The petty cash fund is assigned to a petty cash custodian. (If no petty cash fund, mark this question as "Yes.")				
13. The petty cash fund is reconciled at least once a year by someone other than the custodian. (If no petty cash fund, mark this question as "Yes.")				
14. All disbursements from petty cash are supported by vouchers or receipts. (If no petty cash fund, mark this question as "Yes.")				
15. Wire transfers, EFTs, or transfers between bank accounts are properly authorized by leadership before initiating.				

Payroll	Yes	No	Sometimes	Comments
1. Appropriate leadership approves all pay rates, changes, or bonus payments.				
2. Pay rate changes are documented and maintained in personnel files.				
3. Weekly or biweekly payroll reports (including employees, hours, and rates) are reviewed and approved by someone other than the preparer.				
4. As with other disbursements, the person signing the payroll check is different than the person who prepares the payroll check.				
5. Payroll check totals (including direct deposit and paper checks) are reconciled to the payroll journal by someone other than the preparer.				

	Yes	No	Sometimes	Comments
6. Required payroll tax forms (941, W–2, and other required documents) are filed with appropriate federal and state authorities.				
7. Payroll tax forms (941, W–2, and other required documents) are reconciled to payroll journal by someone other than the payroll preparer.				

Financial Reporting and Reconciliation	Yes	No	Sometimes	Comments
1. Accounting records are current, balanced, and closed monthly.				
2. Financial statements, including balance sheet, income statement, and other relevant financial reports, are prepared monthly.				

3. Financial statements include all funds and account balances, and account balances are reconciled each month.

4. A church officer or board member actively participates in the financial affairs of the church, including reviewing financial reports.

5. An annual budget is prepared and monitored by the church's governing body.

6. The income statement includes a comparison between actual activity and budgeted activity.

7. There is adequate segregation of duties between the authorization, recording, and custody of assets. For example: bank reconciliations are prepared by someone other than the person who deposits cash or writes checks.

SCORING THE ASSESSMENT

To evaluate your assessment, complete the table below and then follow the instructions that follow.

Category	Number of Controls	Number of Controls Operating Effectively (Total "Yes" Responses)	Percentage of Controls Operating Effectively (Divide Column 3 by Column 2 and Multiply by 100)
General Asset Controls	7		
Contributions and Cash Receipts	20		
Payments and Cash Disbursements	15		
Payroll	7		
Financial Reporting and Reconciliation	7		
Total	56		

1. Count the number of "Yes" answers in each category and determine the total for column three. These "Yes" answers represent the controls that are operating consistently and effectively to reduce the risk of fraud or abuse.

   a. If the total score in column three is between 48 and 56: Great job. You have a number of strong controls in place. These controls should help reduce the risk of fraud in your organization. However, there might be a few controls that are not implemented or not consistently followed. Review those controls and determine if you can enhance your processes by implementing these controls.

   b. If the total score is between 37 and 47: Your organization is protected, but still vulnerable. You have some strong controls in place, but some of your processes are still susceptible to fraud or abuse. Some important controls are not being implemented, and these controls will help enhance your processes to safeguard your assets and protect your cash. Review those controls that had a "No" answer and try to implement as many as possible.

   c. If the total score is less than 37: Your organization is vulnerable to fraud and abuse. While you have a few controls in place, your control processes are actually very weak and have exposed your organization to risk. It is important to improve your control processes to properly safeguard your assets and protect your cash. Review those controls that had a "No" answer and work immediately to implement as many of these controls as possible.

2. Now, let's assess how effective your controls are within each category. Fill in the answers for column four. If any category is below 85 percent, the controls within that specific category are not as effective as they can be. As a result, these specific categories are susceptible to fraud and abuse. Refer back to the assessment and review those controls that have not been implemented or not consistently applied. Determine if these controls can be implemented or improved as soon as possible.

PERFORMING AN INTERNAL AUDIT

NCLUDED IN CHAPTER 4 on pages 38–39, there is a chart that describes the characteristics and benefits of two types of audits: an external audit completed by a CPA firm and an internal audit completed by qualified business people within the congregation.

As you have read through chapter 4 and considered the chart of audit options, you may have concluded that your organization doesn't need an external audit at this time. However, you may have determined that having a team of qualified business people to review your financial operations and assess the adequacy of your processes and controls would be helpful.

The following internal audit program is a step-by-step guide that will help your audit team review the key processes in your organization where fraud and abuse occur—including cash and contribution processing, disbursements, credit cards, payroll, and fixed assets. Additionally, the audit team can review other areas that sometimes present problems for churches and nonprofits, like IRS compliance and other governance issues.

Recruit a team of three or four qualified people to perform this review. Assigning specific steps to each person, a team of three or four should be able to complete this audit program in a short amount of time. The audit program gives specific tests for the team to perform and directs the team to review some of the more common processes and procedures where weaknesses often occur in churches and non-profits. This audit program is not meant to be exhaustive, and the audit team should review all areas and processes at your specific organization. The fraud risk assessment in Appendix A may help identify other areas where additional testing and review is needed.

After the team completes the audit program, the team can recommend improvements to the organization's processes based on any errors or weaknesses identified during the audit. I would encourage the audit team to document their results and provide a copy of their results to the leadership team and governing board, who should take appropriate action.

INTERNAL AUDIT PROGRAM FOR CHURCHES AND NONPROFITS

Audit Step	Reviewed By	Results or Comments
Contributions and Cash Receipts		
1. Review the process for receiving and counting cash offerings along with the process to receive, open, and record donations received through the mail. Evaluate facilities, personnel, and the ability to safeguard cash.		
2. Determine if funds are accountable throughout the entire process by evaluating whether cash and checks are handled by at least two people while being received, counted, and deposited into the bank account.		

3. Review the collection of all departmental offerings and contributions to determine if they all follow the same collection, counting, and deposit process.		
4. Review 3–5 weekly count sheets and trace totals from count sheet to daily deposit slips, to general ledger, and to bank statements.		
5. Review the process to identify and record any donor-restricted contributions. Trace restricted contributions to the general ledger and ensure proper segregation.		
6. Review process to issue receipts for donor contributions. Review donor source documents (copies of checks or envelopes) and trace to donor management records.		
7. Determine whether totals from donor records are reconciled to deposits entered in general ledger. Choose one week and trace total donations to donor management records.		
8. Total weekly count sheets and compare to contributions listed on year-to-date financial statements. Research significant discrepancies.		

9. If applicable, determine if the donations of gift cards are accountable and secure by determining the following:		
a. Are gift cards handled by at least two people while being received, counted, and posted to the financial records or logs?		
b. Are gift cards kept in a locked container until used?		
c. Are gift card activities maintained in a log with current balances?		
d. Is gift card usage recorded in the financial records?		
e. Are gift card balances reconciled regularly by someone other than the gift card custodian?		
10. Review the accuracy of the gift card logs. Select ten or twenty gift cards to test. Verify the remaining balance of each gift card with the provider and match each balance on the gift card log.		
11. Review the recording of gift card usage. Trace any purchases made with the gift cards selected in step 10 to the financial records.		

Sales and Accounts Receivable	Reviewed By	Results or Comments
1. If there is sales and accounts receivable activity, select ten customer accounts that have an accounts receivable balance.		
a. Trace sales transactions posted to the customer accounts to supporting sales documentation.		
b. Review the customers' account histories and look for any adjustments that were posted to their accounts.		
c. Review the adjustments and evaluate whether the adjustments were properly supported, reviewed, and approved.		
d. If any adjustments resulted in refunds, review the actual disbursement.		
i. Determine whether the refund was appropriately posted to the customer's credit card or mailed to the customer's address on file.		
ii. If the check has already cleared the bank, review the canceled check to verify that it was written to the customer.		

2. If your financial processes include the ability to post journal entries to the financial records, review any journal entries posted to the accounts receivable general ledger account in the past 12 months for proper support and approval. (An entry posted directly to this account may be an attempt to conceal improper activity.)		
3. Research any unsupported adjustments, refunds, or other questionable transactions.		

Cash Disbursements and Purchasing	Reviewed By	Results or Comments
1. Identify all the bank accounts used by the organization. Determine who has online access and who can sign checks. Evaluate whether these people have the ability to also enter transactions into the general ledger (tests segregation of duties).		
2. Obtain a list of all checks written within the past three months. Select 20 transactions to review, and determine whether each transaction was properly authorized, adequately supported, and posted to the correct account.		

a. For authorization, review purchase requisition / purchase order process or ensure appropriate authorization on invoice. If disbursements are related to contracts, ensure contracts are on file and properly signed.		
b. For support, review receiving reports or approval that services were completed. Match invoices to PO or supporting documents. Verify mathematical accuracy of invoice, timely payment of invoice, proper posting of invoice as paid, and recording of assets in asset system, if applicable.		
3. Obtain canceled checks for the 20 disbursements selected in step 2. (Your bank may provide copies of the check with the monthly bank statement.) Ensure that the payee and amounts agree with the check register. Determine whether the signer on the check was authorized.		
4. Review the process to sign checks. Make sure checks are not signed without reviewing supporting documentation.		

5. Review the numerical sequence of checks issued in the current year and investigate any missing numbers. Identify any checks listed as "void" in the check register and inspect the actual check.		
6. Inspect adequacy of storage facilities for blank check stock, petty cash, and offerings.		
7. Interview the bookkeeping staff to determine if blank checks are ever signed and why.		
8. Review the process to disburse restricted assets (donor-designated contributions). Determine if restricted funds were properly expended according to the donor's wishes.		
9. Review any checks made out to pastors, staff members, or family members for proper support and authorization.		

Credit Card and Charge Accounts	Reviewed By	Results or Comments
1. Obtain list of employees who have access to a business credit card or store charge accounts, and validate their need for this access. Perform this review annually.		

2. For each store charge account, review the invoices for the past three months.		
a. Determine if all receipts were turned in and attached to monthly invoice.		
b. Determine if preapproval was obtained and documented for each purchase.		
c. Review items purchased to determine if they were appropriate and complied with church policy.		
3. Pick three credit card statements to review.		
a. Determine if every transaction is supported by an appropriate receipt or invoice.		
b. Determine if the business purpose of each transaction is clearly identified		
c. For meals and entertainment, determine if the names of those attending are clearly identified.		
d. Determine if each expense was charged to the appropriate general ledger account.		
e. Determine if credit card purchases are reviewed and approved by an appropriate supervisor.		

Petty Cash	Reviewed By	Results or Comments
1. Count all petty cash funds and determine if funds are intact.		
2. Determine if the petty cash fund is assigned to custodian.		
3. Determine if the petty cash fund is reconciled at least once a year by someone other than the custodian.		
4. Review a recent fund replenishment and examine receipts for compliance with established policy.		

Payroll	Reviewed By	Results or Comments
1. Review each employee's personnel file. Determine whether a properly completed Form W–4 and I–9 is on file for each employee. Ensure each form is properly dated and signed.		
2. Choose one or more employees and compare actual rates of pay with rates authorized by the church leadership. Examine withholdings and deductions from paycheck and trace to W–4 and other documents authorizing voluntary deductions.		

3. Trace weekly payroll to actual disbursements made (paper check and direct deposit) and to posting in general ledger.		
4. Review how minister's pay is handled. For example, W–2 versus 1099; Social Security is not withheld, but minister can make voluntary withholding payments. Seek guidance from a qualified CPA, if necessary.		
5. Compare a few W–2s issued at year-end to quarterly reports and payroll records. Research any discrepancies.		
6. Ensure that quarterly Forms 941 are properly submitted (for reporting and paying federal income and FICA taxes withheld). Ensure similar state forms are filed, if necessary.		
7. Review the Form 941 submissions for the past year. Evaluate the completeness of each submission by tracing the figures on the report to applicable payroll reports for the same period.		

8. Sign up with the Treasury Department's Electronic Federal Tax Payment System. Assign someone not involved in the payroll process to visit the system on a regular basis to make sure tax deposits are being made.		

Bank Activity and Reconciliations	Reviewed By	Results or Comments
1. Review process to reconcile bank accounts each month.		
a. Pick one month and trace "bank balance" to bank statement. Next trace "book balance" to general ledger and current financial report.		
b. Verify reconciling items (deposits in transit, outstanding checks) by tracing to next subsequent bank statement.		
c. Research any outstanding check that doesn't clear by next statement and any unusual reconciling items carried forward from previous months.		
2. Determine if the person who reconciles the bank statements is authorized to sign checks.		

3. Verify that bank reconciliations are performed completely and completed in the time expected.		
4. Review the process for electronic fund transfers and wire transfers. Review bank statements and trace 3–5 electronic transfers and/or withdrawals for proper approval, support, and posting.		
a. For approval, ensure proper segregation of duties.		
b. For support, trace transaction to invoice, purchase order, etc.		
c. For posting, trace transaction from bank statement to general ledger.		

Financial Statement Review	Reviewed By	Results or Comments
1. Evaluate the adequacy of monthly financial statements. Do they include balance sheet, income statement, and cash flow, if necessary?		
2. Evaluate the balance sheet. Agree the balances of all checking and savings accounts, CDs, etc., as listed on financial statements to supporting bank statements. Research any significant discrepancies. Determine if earnings and losses are recorded in the financial records.		

3. Test a sample of account balances on the financial statements and agree balances to general ledger. Make sure ending balances agree with beginning balances in subsequent period.		
4. Obtain year-end statements for any mortgages or loans and determine that the correct balance is reported on the financial statements. Determine if payments are current.		
5. Review a schedule of unpaid invoices, and determine if there are any items significantly past due.		
6. Determine if AP totals are properly listed in the financial statements.		

Property and Insurance	Reviewed By	Results or Comments
1. Determine whether the church maintains an up-to-date inventory record of noncash assets, fixed assets, buildings, and equipment. Select 10 items on the list and visually inspect the items.		
2. Determine whether periodic reviews are performed to test the accuracy of the fixed asset inventory records. Evaluate the adequacy of those reviews.		

3. Examine the titles and/or deeds to land, buildings, and vehicles.		
4. Examine current insurance policies for dates and amounts to evaluate whether adequate coverage exists. Determine if all major property and equipment is covered.		
5. Determine if the church is carrying workers' compensation insurance as required by law (if applicable).		

IRS Compliance	Reviewed By	Results or Comments
1. Determine if payments made to contractors are properly accumulated and reported on Form 1099 when totaling $600 or more.		
2. Determine if ministerial housing allowances are properly approved and recorded in the board minutes at the beginning of each year.		
3. Determine if Form 990-T is properly filed, if necessary.		
4. If church doesn't have an accountable reimbursement plan, ensure appropriate expense reimbursements are accumulated and added to the staff W–2s at year-end.		

5. Review year-end giving receipts for compliance with IRS regulations ensuring tax deductibility.		
6. Ensure acknowledgments are sent for all single contributions of $250 or more.		
7. If no goods or services were provided (other than intangible religious benefits) in exchange for a gift, include in the receipt a statement to this effect.		

ENDNOTES

CHAPTER 1: FRAUD RISK: WHAT EVERY LEADER NEEDS TO KNOW

1. Associated Press, "Father and Son Pastors Plead Guilty to Stealing $3.1 M from Church," FoxNews.com, June 15, 2009, accessed September 26, 2013, http://www.foxnews.com/story/2009/06/15/father-and-son-pastors-plead-guilty-to-stealing–31-m-from-church/.

2. "Former Central Texas Minister Sentenced in $700,000 Theft," KWTX.com, October 1, 2008, accessed September 26, 2013, http://www.kwtx.com/news/headlines/30183349.html.

3. Samuel Smith, "BGCT Reports $1.3M Fraud, Mismanagement in Church Funds," BPNews.net, November 1, 2006, accessed September 26, 2013, http://www.bpnews.net/bpnews.asp?ID=24299.

4. Association of Certified Fraud Examiners, *Report to the Nations on Occupational Fraud and Abuse: 2014 Global Fraud Study*, 2, 24, accessed March 12, 2015, http://www.acfe.com/rttn/docs/2014-report-to-nations.pdf.

5. Ibid., 5.

6. Ibid., 24.

7. Internal Revenue Service, *Internal Revenue Service Fiscal Year 2012 Enforcement and Service Results*, 7, accessed July 26, 2013, http://www.irs.gov/uac/Newsroom/FY–2012-Enforcement-and-Service-Results.

8. The United States Senate Committee on Finance, "Grassley Releases Review of Tax Issues Raised by Media-based Ministries," January 6, 2011, accessed April 14, 2011, http://www.finance. senate.gov/newsroom/ranking/release/?id=5fa343ed–87eb–49b0 –82b9–28a9502910f7.

CHAPTER 2: INTERNAL CONTROL AND RISK MANAGEMENT

1. Warren Bird, *The Economic Outlook of Very Large Churches* (Leadership Network, 2013), 3, accessed June 27, 2015, http:// leadnet.org/the_economic_outlook_of_very_large_churches_pdf/.
2. Christopher T. Marquet, *The 2013 Marquet Report on Embezzlement* (Marquet International, 2014), 24, accessed March 12, 2015, http://www.marquetinternational.com/trackpdfs/ the_2013_marquet_report_on_embezzlement.pdf?track=185684.
3. Association of Certified Fraud Examiners, *Report to the Nations: 2014,* 59.
4. Assemblies of God USA, "Our Mission & Core Values," last modified February 26, 2010, accessed July 29, 2013, http://www .ag.org/top/About/mission.cfm.
5. KPMG LLP, *Who Is the Typical Fraudster?,* 10, accessed February 20, 2013, http://www.kpmg.com/US/en/IssuesAndInsights/ ArticlesPublications/Documents/who-is-the-typical-fraudster.PDF.
6. Ibid., 15–16.
7. Ibid., 10, 13.
8. Association of Certified Fraud Examiners, *Report to the Nations: 2014,* 2, 4–5, 25.
9. Ibid., 2, 24.
10. Ibid., 24, 28.
11. Ibid., 4.
12. Ibid., 58.
13. Ibid., 19.
14. Ibid.

15. Ibid., 5, 25.

16. Association of Certified Fraud Examiners, *Report to the Nations on Occupational Fraud and Abuse: 2012 Global Fraud Study*, 5, accessed May 23, 2013, http://www.acfe.com/uploadedFiles/ACFE_Website/Content/rttn/2012-report-to-nations.pdf.

17. Association of Certified Fraud Examiners, *Report to the Nations: 2014*, 4.

18. National Center For Charitable Statistics, "Quick Facts About Nonprofits," accessed March 12, 2015, http://nccs.urban.org/statistics/quickfacts.cfm.

19. Association of Certified Fraud Examiners, *Report to the Nations: 2014*, 4.

20. David K. Shipler, "Reagan and Gorbachev Sign Missile Treaty and Vow to Work for Greater Reductions," NYTimes.com, December 9, 1987, accessed August 24, 2013, http://www.nytimes.com/1987/12/09/politics/09REAG.html?pagewanted=2&pagewanted=all&smid=pl-share.

21. COSO is an acronym for the Committee of Sponsoring Organizations for the Commission on Fraudulent Financial Reporting (Treadway Commission).

22. Kurt F. Reding et al., *Internal Auditing: Assurance & Consulting Services* (Altamonte Springs, FL: The Institute of Internal Auditors Research Foundation, 2007), 5–8.

CHAPTER 3: MOVING FORWARD AFTER FRAUD

1. Paul Payne, "Guerneville Woman Takes Plea Bargain in Church Embezzlement Case," PressDemocrat.com, March 12, 2012, accessed July 29, 2013, http://www.pressdemocrat.com/article/20120312/articles/120319932?tc=ar.

2. Sharon Otterman and Russ Buettner, "In Million-Dollar Theft Case, Church Worker with a Secret Past," NYTimes.com, January 30, 2012, accessed July 29, 2013, http://www.nytimes .com/2012/01/31/nyregion/new-york-archdiocese-bookkeeper -charged-with-stealing–1-million.html?_r=4&pagewanted=all&.
3. Federal Bureau of Investigation, "Former American Diabetes Financial Analyst Pleads Guilty to Embezzling Nearly $570,000," FBI Washington Field Office, September 23, 2011, accessed July 29, 2013, http://www.fbi.gov/washingtondc/press-releases/2011/ former-american-diabetes-financial-analyst-pleads-guilty-to -embezzling-nearly–570–000.
4. Jeff German, "Former Las Vegas Church Treasurer Faces Fraud Charges," ReviewJournal.com, September 6, 2012, accessed June 10, 2013, http://www.reviewjournal.com/news/crime-courts/ former-las-vegas-church-treasurer-faces-fraud-charges.
5. Richard R. Hammar, "If an Embezzler Confesses," *Managing Your Church Blog*, August 11, 2011, accessed August 26, 2011, http://blog.managingyourchurch.com/2011/08/if_an_embezzler _confesses.html.
6. Richard R. Hammar, "How Do We Confront Suspected Embezzlement?" ChurchLawandTax.com, accessed December 21, 2011, http://www.churchlawandtax.com/private/library/ viewarticle.php?aid=118.
7. Ibid.
8. Association of Certified Fraud Examiners, *Report to the Nations: 2014,* 58.
9. Ibid., 64, 66.
10. Ibid., 65.
11. Ibid., 66.
12. Ibid., 67.
13. Ibid., 65.

CHAPTER 4: TOOLS TO REDUCE THE RISK OF FRAUD

1. Ibid., 19.
2. Evangelical Council for Financial Accountability, "ECFA Mission Statement," accessed August 28, 2013, http://www.ecfa.org/Content/MissionStatement.
3. The ECFA *Seven Standards of Responsible Stewardship* is used with permission from Michael Martin, Director of Member Services and Legal Counsel, ECFA.

CASE STUDY 1: SKIMMING DONATIONS

1. Association of Certified Fraud Examiners, *Report to the Nations: 2014*, 17, 29.

CASE STUDY 2: SECRET BANK ACCOUNT

1. KPMG, *Who is the Typical Fraudster?*, 10.
2. Ibid.
3. Federal Bureau of Investigation, "Head of Charter School Pleads Guilty to Fraud Charges," FBI Philadelphia Division, August 13, 2013, accessed August 13, 2013, http://www.fbi.gov/philadelphia/press-releases/2013/head-of-charter-school-pleads-guilty-to-fraud-charges.

CASE STUDY 3: WRITING BLANK CHECKS

1. The names of the organization and individuals involved have been changed to protect their identities.

2. Federal Bureau of Investigation, "Bookkeeper Sentenced to Prison for Fraud and Aggravated Identity Theft," FBI Birmingham Division, April 3, 2013, accessed April 3, 2013, http://www.fbi .gov/birmingham/press-releases/2013/bookkeeper-sentenced-to -prison-for-fraud-and-aggravated-identity-theft.
3. Marquet, *2013 Marquet Report*, 6.
4. Association of Certified Fraud Examiners, *Report to the Nations: 2014*, 29.
5. Ibid., 17.

CASE STUDY 6: ELECTRONIC FUND TRANSFERS

1. Federal Bureau of Investigation, "Former American Diabetes Financial Analyst Pleads Guilty."
2. Federal Bureau of Investigation, "Landover Woman Indicted for Allegedly Embezzling More Than $453,000 from Her Employer," FBI Baltimore Division, April 29, 2013, accessed July 29, 2013, http://www.fbi.gov/baltimore/press-releases/2013/ landover-woman-indicted-for-allegedly-embezzling-more- than-453-000-from-her-employer.

CASE STUDY 8: CREDIT CARD REFUNDS

1. Association of Certified Fraud Examiners, *Report to the Nations: 2014*, 13.
2. Ibid., 13, 17.
3. Ibid., 29.

CASE STUDY 9: UNPAID PAYROLL TAXES

1. Marquet, *2013 Marquet Report*, 8.

2. Will Astor, "Plea Sets Payback by Sykes," RBJ.net, November 4, 2011, accessed September 26, 2013, http://www.rbj.net/ print_article.asp?aID=189432.

3. "Federal Money Laundering, Tax Fraud Charges," SteubenCourier.com, October 31, 2011, accessed September 26, 2013, http://www.steubencourier.com/x1138515272/ Federal-money-laundering-tax-fraud-charges.

4. Internal Revenue Service, "Examples of Employment Tax Fraud Investigations—Fiscal Year 2012," updated September 17, 2013, accessed September 26, 2013, http://www.irs.gov/uac/Examples -of-Employment-Tax-Fraud-Investigations-Fiscal-Year–2012.

CASE STUDY 10: PETTY CASH AND TUITION PAYMENTS

1. Association of Certified Fraud Examiners, *Report to the Nations: 2014*, 13, 17.

2. Ibid., 29.

3. Ibid., 13.

4. Ibid., 13, 17.

5. Ibid., 29.

CASE STUDY 11: MISSING ASSETS

1. Ibid., 13, 29.

2. Ibid., 17.

CASE STUDY 12: EXTRA PAYROLL CHECKS

1. Ibid., 13, 17.

2. Ibid., 29.